Country Woman

Pasta, please

Edited by Annette Gohlke

Associate Editor: Joan Sobczak

Illustration/Layout Artist: Janet Kumbier

Production: Sally Manich, Sue Flower

Cover Photography by Mike Huibregtse

Library of Congress Catalog Card Number: 82-50005
ISBN: 0-89821-042-9

5925 Country Lane
Suite 1977, Box 612
Milwaukee, WI 53201

From Our Country Kitchen...

Dear Friends:

Country cooks put noodles in dishes from salads to desserts. In gathering and selecting the recipes for this book, we found they even take "ordinary" dishes like casseroles or noodle bakes and add innovative ingredients to make them extraordinary!

Pasta, Please is chock-full of the best recipes entered in the *Country Woman* pasta recipe contest. We're sure you'll find plenty of new recipes to make with a variety of noodles now that you have this cookbook.

Side dishes you can make on the stovetop dress up any main dish you have in the oven. Noodles can also put a little surprise into fruit or vegetable salads, and pasta desserts top off any meal in a way that's anything but ho-hum.

If you've found yourself preparing the same casserole whenever you need a quick, one-dish meal, you'll find ideas for deliciously *different* casseroles in *Pasta, Please*...including a whole chapter of casseroles that go a long way at the table but require only a short time in the kitchen.

Or try jumbo noodles stuffed with tasty fillings that are sure to be a big hit with family or guests. To give lasagna lovers some enticing, new tastes, try the layered noodle bakes in *Pasta, Please*.

As you page through *Pasta, Please*, you'll find recipes that use pasta in all shapes and sizes. Some of the recipes just call for novelty noodles and leave it up to you to choose bow tie, sea shell, corkscrew or whatever type of noodle you'd like.

So have fun preparing the recipes in *Pasta, Please*, and then enjoy pleasing your family with new and *interesting* noodle dishes!

Grace Howaniec

Grace Howaniec
Country Woman Food Editor

Contents

Quick
Casseroles

Meaty Mixables

ROTINI SALISICCIA

3 quarts water
2 tablespoons plus 1-1/2
teaspoons salt, divided
1 teaspoon plus 3 tablespoons
butter, divided
12 ounces rotini OR elbow
macaroni
1-1/2 pounds Italian sausage, cut
into 1/2-in. slices
1-1/2 cups mushrooms, sliced
1/3 cup green pepper, chopped
1/3 cup onion, minced
1/2 cup flour
1 teaspoon sweet basil
1 teaspoon dry mustard
4 cups milk
6 ounces mozzarella cheese,
shredded
6 ounces Swiss cheese,
shredded
1 tablespoon Worcestershire
sauce
1/4 cup parsley, chopped

Bring 3 quarts water to which 2 tablespoons salt and 1 teaspoon butter have been added to a boil. Cook rotini to AL DENTE state. In large skillet brown sausage over medium-high heat. Remove from skillet. Add 3 tablespoons butter to sausage drippings. Saute mushrooms, green pepper and onion in drippings until tender. Remove skillet from heat. Stir in flour, 1-1/2 teaspoons salt, basil and dry mustard. Gradually blend in milk, 1 cup at a time. Return to heat; cook, stirring, until sauce thickens. Blend in cheeses and Worcestershire sauce. Reduce heat to low. Cook, stirring, until cheese melts. Combine rotini, sausage, parsley and sauce. Spread in 4-quart casserole or 2 smaller baking dishes. Bake covered at 350° for 25 to 30 minutes. Garnish with additional parsley, if desired. Serves 8.

—**Florence Lorence, Racine, Wisconsin**

CHOP SUEY CASSEROLE

1 pound ground beef
1 cup celery, diced
1 medium onion, chopped
1/4 cup green pepper, chopped
1 10-3/4-ounce can tomato soup
1 4-ounce can mushrooms,
drained
1 16-ounce can chop suey
vegetables, undrained
1 tablespoon soy sauce, optional
4 ounces thin spaghetti, partially
cooked, drained
3/4 cup cheddar cheese, grated

Brown ground beef with celery, onion and green pepper. Drain off fat. Add remaining ingredients EXCEPT spaghetti and cheese; cook 10 minutes. Combine meat mixture and spaghetti; pour into 12- x 8-in. baking dish. Top with cheese; bake for 45 minutes at 350°. **Note:** Casserole may be frozen unbaked. —**Pat Vandenbusche, Metamora, Ohio**

INSIDE-OUT RAVIOLI

1 pound ground beef
1/2 cup onion, chopped
1 clove garlic, minced
1 10-ounce package frozen, chopped spinach, cooked, drained
Liquid from cooking spinach plus Water to make 1 cup
1 16-ounce jar spaghetti sauce with mushrooms

1 8-ounce can tomato sauce
1/2 teaspoon salt
Dash pepper
2 cups shell OR elbow macaroni, cooked, drained
1 cup mozzarella cheese, shredded
1/2 cup soft bread crumbs
2 eggs, beaten
1/4 cup oil

Saute ground beef, onion and garlic in large skillet. When meat has browned, drain fat. Add spinach liquid plus water, spaghetti sauce, tomato sauce, salt and pepper to meat mixture. Simmer 10 minutes. Combine spinach, macaroni, cheese, bread crumbs, eggs and oil; place into 13- x 9- x 2-in. baking dish. Top with meat sauce. Bake at 350° for 30 minutes; let stand 10 minutes before serving. Serves 8. **—Kathryn Worth, Waukon, Iowa**

GREEN NOODLE CASSEROLE

1 cup onion, finely chopped
2 tablespoons celery tops, chopped
2 tablespoons cooking oil
1 pound veal, cubed
1/2 to 1 teaspoon paprika
1 cup chicken stock
8 ounces spinach noodles

4-1/2 ounces mushrooms, fresh OR canned
1 10-3/4-ounce can cream of chicken soup
1 tablespoon poppy seed, optional
1/2 teaspoon salt
1/8 teaspoon pepper

Saute onion and celery in oil until soft but not brown. Add veal and paprika to taste; brown lightly. Add stock; simmer covered for 30 minutes. Meanwhile, cook spinach noodles according to package directions; drain. Combine all ingredients. Bake uncovered in 2-quart casserole about 40 minutes at 350°. Serves 4. **—Margaret Zickert, Deerfield, Wisconsin**

DRIED BEEF CASSEROLE

1 10-3/4-ounce can cream of mushroom soup
1-1/2 cups milk
1 cup elbow macaroni, uncooked

3 tablespoons onion, chopped
1/4 pound dried beef
1 cup mild cheese (Velveeta or other)
2 hard-cooked eggs, diced

Combine soup and milk; stir in remaining ingredients. Place into greased, 2-quart casserole; chill overnight. Bake uncovered at 350° for 1 hour, stirring halfway through baking time. **—Marie Showalter, Hagerstown, Maryland**

MAZETTI

1 pound ground veal
1 pound ground pork
1 green pepper, finely chopped
1 onion, minced
1 stalk celery, chopped
2 tablespoons butter
8 ounces medium egg noodles,
  cooked, drained

1 10-3/4-ounce can tomato soup
1 10-3/4-ounce can cream of
  chicken soup
1 4-ounce can mushrooms, drained
Salt and pepper to taste
8 ounces Old English cheese, grated

Saute meats, green pepper, onion and celery in butter until meats are browned. Combine cooked noodles, meats and vegetables, soups and mushrooms. Sprinkle with salt and pepper. Place into a large casserole; top with grated cheese. Bake at 350° for 45 minutes.

—Edith Diedrick, LaSalle, Illinois

PASTITSIO

Meat Sauce:
1-1/2 pounds ground beef
1 cup onion, chopped
1 16-ounce can tomatoes,
  undrained

1 6-ounce can tomato paste
1/2 teaspoon dried thyme,
  crushed
1 teaspoon salt

Pasta and Cheese:
4 egg whites, slightly beaten
1/2 cup American OR feta cheese,
  cubed

2 cups elbow macaroni,
  cooked, drained

Milk Sauce:
1/2 cup butter
1/2 cup flour
1/2 teaspoon cinnamon

1 teaspoon salt
4 cups milk
4 egg yolks, slightly beaten

Meat Sauce: Saute beef and onion until meat is browned; drain off fat. Add undrained tomatoes, tomato paste, thyme and 1 teaspoon salt. Simmer covered for 30 minutes, stirring frequently. **Pasta and Cheese:** Stir egg whites and cheese into cooked, drained macaroni. Blend in meat sauce. Turn into 13- x 9- x 2-in. baking dish. **Milk Sauce:** In large saucepan melt butter. Blend in flour, cinnamon and 1 teaspoon salt. Add milk all at once; cook, stirring constantly, until thick and bubbly. Remove from heat. Gradually stir part of milk sauce into egg yolks; blend well. Add yolk mixture to remaining milk sauce, stirring rapidly. Pour over contents of baking dish; sprinkle lightly with more cinnamon, if desired. Bake at 375° for 35 to 40 minutes. Let stand 10 minutes before serving. Serves 12.

—Dianna Etchison, Frankton, Indiana

ZESTY PIZZA CASSEROLE

1 pound ground beef, browned, drained
2 8-ounce cans pizza sauce OR 2 cups sauce below
1 4-ounce can sliced mushrooms, undrained
1 teaspoon oregano OR to taste
1 teaspoon garlic salt

2 cups rotini noodles, cooked, drained
2/3 cup milk
8 ounces mozzarella cheese, shredded
Salami, cherry tomatoes, parsley, optional

Sauce:

2 6-ounce cans tomato paste
2 8-ounce cans tomato sauce
1 medium onion, minced

1 teaspoon salt
1 teaspoon oregano
1/4 teaspoon garlic powder

To browned, drained beef add pizza sauce, mushrooms and liquid from can, oregano and garlic salt. Bring to boil; remove from heat. Combine rotini and milk. Into a 2-quart casserole place half of meat sauce, topped with half of rotini mixture, then 4 ounces cheese. Repeat layers. Bake covered at 350° for 25 to 30 minutes. Garnish with salami, cherry tomatoes and parsley, if desired. **Note:** Macaroni may be used instead of rotini. Serves 6.

—Sherrill Libby, Levant, Maine

CORNED BEEF CASSEROLE

3 cups noodles, cooked, drained
1 12-ounce can corned beef, chopped
4 ounces sharp cheddar cheese, shredded

1 10-3/4-ounce can cream of chicken soup
1 cup milk
1/2 cup onion, chopped
3/4 cup bread crumbs
1/4 cup butter, melted

Thoroughly combine all ingredients EXCEPT bread crumbs and butter. Fold into greased, 3-quart casserole. Combine bread crumbs and melted butter; mix with fork. Sprinkle buttered crumbs over top of casserole. Bake at 350° about 45 minutes.

—Elaine Brown, Prumzurlay, West Germany (APO, New York)

HASH CASSEROLE

1 15-ounce can corned beef hash
1 10-3/4-ounce can cream of mushroom soup

1 cup cheddar cheese, shredded
4 ounces shell macaroni, cooked, drained

Combine all ingredients; place into 2-quart casserole. Bake at 350° until golden brown and bubbly. —**Dianne Herfurth, Vinemont, Alabama**

Vegetable Bounty

ZUCCHINI CASSEROLE

2 cups zucchini, sliced
1 small onion, sliced
1 carrot, chopped
1 12-ounce can tuna fish
2 cups egg noodles, cooked, drained

1 10-3/4-ounce can cream of mushroom soup
1 cup sour cream
1/2 teaspoon dill seed
Dash salt and pepper
1/2 cup dry bread crumbs
2 tablespoons butter

Parboil zucchini, onion and carrot for 10 minutes in salted water. Drain. Place vegetables into greased, 1-quart casserole. Fold in tuna and cooked noodles. Combine soup, sour cream, dill seed, salt and pepper; pour over casserole. Top with bread crumbs dotted with butter. Bake at 350° for 30 minutes. **—Carol L. Shiveler, Swedesboro, New Jersey**

SAUERKRAUT AND MACARONI CASSEROLE

1 16-ounce can sauerkraut
3 large onions, chopped
2 green peppers, chopped
16 ounces fresh mushrooms, sliced
1/2 pound bacon

16 ounces spiral macaroni, cooked, drained
1 10-3/4-ounce can beef stock
1 10-3/4-ounce can cream of mushroom soup

Cook sauerkraut about 30 minutes. Saute onion, green pepper, mushrooms and bacon together. Add to sauerkraut. Stir in cooked macaroni. Combine beef stock and cream of mushroom soup. Blend into sauerkraut mixture. Place into a casserole dish; bake at 325° for 1 hour. **Note:** Any type of gravy may be used instead of the beef stock and mushroom soup mixture.

—Irene Staebell, Corfu, New York

NOODLES IN NO TIME

8 ounces egg noodles, cooked, drained
1 10-ounce package frozen cauliflower, partially thawed, cut up
1 10-ounce package frozen, chopped broccoli, partially thawed

1 10-3/4-ounce can cream of mushroom soup
1 cup sour cream
1 medium onion, chopped
1-1/2 cups muenster OR cheddar cheese, shredded

To cooked noodles add remaining ingredients. Mix gently. Fold into a 13- x 9-in. baking dish; bake at 350° for 30 to 45 minutes or until bubbly and hot.
—Anna-Margaret Binder, Port Allegany, Pennsylvania

VEGETARIAN CASSEROLE

2 cups onion, chopped
2 cups celery with leaves, chopped
1-1/2 cups carrots, grated
2 tablespoons oil
2 28-ounce cans Italian whole tomatoes
1 16-ounce can peeled, crushed tomatoes
1/8 teaspoon oregano
2 tablespoons salt
1-1/2 teaspoons pepper
1 teaspoon garlic powder
24 ounces bow tie, shell OR elbow macaroni, cooked, drained
2 10-ounce packages frozen, chopped spinach, slightly thawed
1 cup Parmesan cheese, grated

In large saucepan saute onion, celery and carrots in oil about 5 minutes. Stir in tomatoes, oregano, salt, pepper and garlic; bring to a boil. Reduce heat; simmer 1 hour. When sauce is ready, stir in cooked noodles; add spinach. Mix thoroughly; spoon into 2 baking pans. Sprinkle with cheese; bake at 350° for 30 minutes. **Note:** One of the UNBAKED casseroles may be frozen to use as a quick meal later. The mixture will also keep for a day or two in the refrigerator if prepared ahead of time.

—Helen F. DiCicco, Brockton, Massachusetts

CREAMED CORN CASSEROLE

3/4 pound ground veal
3/4 pound ground pork
1/4 cup green pepper, finely chopped
Salt and pepper to taste
1 16-ounce can creamed corn
4 ounces noodles, cooked, drained
1 cup cheese, grated, divided
Cornflake crumbs

Brown meats with green pepper, salt and pepper. Stir in creamed corn. Add cooked pasta to meat mixture; stir in 1/2 cup grated cheese. Place mixture into a 2-quart casserole; top with remaining cheese and cornflake crumbs. Bake at 350° for 30 minutes.

—Phyllis Visser, Uxbridge, Massachusetts

NOODLE-RICE CASSEROLE

1/2 cup butter
8 ounces very thin noodles
2 cups quick rice
2 13-3/4 ounce cans chicken broth
2 10-3/4 ounce cans onion soup
1 8-ounce can sliced water chestnuts, drained
1 tablespoon soy sauce
1/2 cup water

In large saucepan melt butter. Add uncooked noodles; cook, stirring, until lightly browned. Add uncooked rice and remaining ingredients. Mix well; turn into 13- x 9- x 2-in. baking dish. Bake at 350° for 35 to 40 minutes.

—Ann Kuhn, Naperville, Illinois

SPINACH 'N' SPAGHETTI

1 egg, beaten
1/2 cup dairy sour cream
1/4 cup milk
1/4 cup Parmesan cheese, grated, divided
2 teaspoons dried onion
1/2 teaspoon salt
Dash pepper

2 cups Monterey Jack cheese, shredded
1 10-ounce package frozen, chopped spinach, cooked, drained
4 ounces spaghetti, cooked, drained

Combine egg, cream, milk, 2 tablespoons Parmesan, onion, salt and pepper; mix well. Stir in Monterey Jack cheese. Fold in spinach and spaghetti. Turn mixture into ungreased, 10- x 6- x 2-in. baking dish. Sprinkle with remaining 2 tablespoons Parmesan. Bake covered 15 minutes at 350°, then uncovered 15 to 20 minutes more or until heated through.

—Janice Rinne, Stockton, California

Dairy Delights

COTTAGE CHEESE 'N' NOODLES

2 cups small curd, cream-style cottage cheese
1 8-ounce carton French onion dip
1 egg
4 tablespoons Parmesan cheese, grated, divided

3 tablespoons dried onion
1 teaspoon onion salt
Pepper to taste
8 ounces medium-width egg noodles, cooked, drained
2 tablespoons poppy seeds

Combine cottage cheese, dip, egg, 3 tablespoons cheese, onion, onion salt and pepper. Add to cooked noodles. Fold mixture into greased, oblong, 2-quart baking dish. Sprinkle poppy seeds and 1 tablespoon cheese over top of casserole. Bake at 350° for 25 to 30 minutes. Serves 4.

—Theresa Farris, Detroit, Michigan

CHEESY SURPRISE

24 ounces noodles, cooked, drained
2 10-3/4-ounce cans cream of shrimp soup
1-2/3 cups evaporated milk

3 cups Velveeta cheese, diced
1/2 4-1/2-ounce can sliced, ripe olives
1/2 2-ounce jar pimento, chopped
1 cup milk

Thoroughly combine all ingredients. Bake in 5-quart Dutch oven for 50 minutes at 350°. **Note:** A small can of shrimp may be added for extra flavor. Serves 6.

—Maryette Sturm, Sebeka, Minnesota

TASTY CHEESE-PASTA CASSEROLE

1-1/2 pounds ground beef plus
    1/2 pound bulk Italian
    sausage, browned, drained
2 medium onions, diced
1 clove garlic, crushed
1 14-ounce jar spaghetti sauce
1 16-ounce can stewed tomatoes

1 4-ounce can sliced mushrooms,
    drained
8 ounces large shell macaroni,
    cooked, drained
3 cups sour cream
8 ounces provolone cheese, sliced
8 ounces mozzarella cheese, sliced

To drained meat add onion, garlic, spaghetti sauce, tomatoes and mushrooms; simmer 20 minutes. Spoon half of cooked noodles into deep casserole; top with half of meat sauce, half of sour cream and all the provolone cheese. Repeat layers, but end with mozzarella cheese. Bake covered at 350° for 35 minutes, then uncovered for a few minutes more.

—Anna R. Dittler, Sterling, Colorado

DOUBLE-GOOD MACARONI AND CHEESE

8 ounces macaroni, cooked,
    drained
16 ounces cream-style cottage
    cheese
8 ounces cheddar cheese,
    grated

1 cup sour cream
1 egg, beaten
1 tablespoon onion
1 teaspoon salt
1/8 teaspoon pepper
1-1/2 tablespoons wheat germ

While cooking macaroni, combine cheeses, sour cream, egg, onion and salt and pepper. Fold hot macaroni gently into cheese mixture. Spoon into greased, 2-quart casserole; sprinkle with wheat germ. Bake at 350° for 45 minutes.

—Marion Pool, Groom, Texas

SPAGHETTI PUFF

1 cup milk, scalded
1/4 cup butter, melted
3 egg yolks, beaten
1-1/2 cups spaghetti, broken,
    cooked, drained
1-1/2 cups sharp process American
    cheese, grated
2/3 cup dry bread crumbs

1/4 cup onion, chopped
1 tablespoon parsley, snipped
1 tablespoon pimento,
    chopped
1 teaspoon Worcestershire
    sauce
1/2 teaspoon salt
3 egg whites, stiffly beaten

Combine scalded milk and melted butter. Gradually stir hot mixture into egg yolks. Add spaghetti and remaining ingredients EXCEPT egg whites; mix thoroughly. Fold in egg whites; pour into greased, 12- x 8- x 2-in. baking dish. Bake at 325° for 1 hour or until set. Serves 8.

—Dora E. Rupnow, Jefferson, Wisconsin

FETTUCCINE A LA ROMANA

16 ounces extra-wide noodles, cooked, drained
1/4 cup butter
1/2 cup Parmesan cheese, grated, divided
Salt and pepper to taste

2 2-1/2-ounce packages Buddig sliced ham, diced
1 8-1/2-ounce can early small peas
1 cup whipping cream

In a casserole dish add butter to drained noodles. Blend in 1/4 cup grated cheese and salt and pepper to taste. Add meat and peas; mix well. Dot with butter; sprinkle with remaining cheese. Pour whipping cream over top; bake at 350° for 40 minutes. Serves 4.   **—Susan Gallo Bourquin, Warren, Illinois**

Fish 'n' Fowl Favorites

TUNA TIME

Loaf:

4 eggs, slightly beaten
1/2 cup sliced olives
2 tablespoons onion, grated
1 12-ounce can tuna fish

1 cup soft bread crumbs
2-1/4 cups macaroni, cooked, drained
1/4 cup butter, melted

Sauce:

1 13-ounce can evaporated milk
1/2 teaspoon salt
1 teaspoon dry mustard

1 tablespoon horseradish
2 cups Velveeta cheese

Loaf: Combine all ingredients. **Sauce:** Combine all ingredients; cook over low heat just until cheese melts. Add sauce to loaf ingredients; combine thoroughly. Divide mixture into 2 loaf pans. Bake uncovered for 50 to 60 minutes at 325°. Serve hot or sliced cold for sandwiches.

—Gail M. Schutz, White Hall, Illinois

CHICKEN-SPAGHETTI DELIGHT

4 strips bacon
2 onions, chopped
2 cloves garlic, crushed
1 4-ounce can chopped mushrooms, drained
2 8-ounce cans tomato sauce
1 5-1/3-ounce can evaporated milk

16 ounces spaghetti, cooked, drained
1 3-pound chicken, boiled, boned, cubed
16 ounces cheese, grated
1 2-ounce jar pimento, chopped
Salt to taste

Fry bacon; remove from pan. Saute onion, garlic and mushrooms in fat. Add tomato sauce and milk. Combine spaghetti, tomato mixture, chicken and cheese; add pimento and crumbled bacon. Salt to taste. Bake at 300° about 30 minutes in a 13- x 9-in. baking pan. Serves 8. **—Fern Porter, Atlanta, Texas**

CHICKEN-AVOCADO CASSEROLE

6 ounces spaghetti, broken, cooked, drained
1 10-3/4-ounce can cream of chicken soup
1 soup can water
1/4 cup pimento, finely chopped
2 tablespoons butter
1-1/2 cups chicken, cooked, diced
1 cup avocado, seeded, skinned, cubed
1/2 cup Parmesan cheese, grated
1/3 cup buttered bread crumbs

Place cooked spaghetti into 1-1/2-quart casserole. In small saucepan combine soup, water, pimento, butter and chicken. Bring to boil over moderate heat. Pour soup mixture over spaghetti; toss until noodles are well coated. Fold in avocado cubes; top with cheese and buttered bread crumbs. Bake at 350º for 20 to 25 minutes or until bubbly. Serves 6.

—Sally R. Place, Chestertown, New York

NOODLE-TUNA CASSEROLE

8 ounces noodles, cooked, drained
2 6-1/2-ounce cans light chunk tuna
1 cup Velveeta cheese, cubed
1 14-1/2-ounce can cut asparagus spears, drained
1 4-ounce can mushroom pieces, drained
1 8-ounce can water chestnuts, drained, chopped, optional
1 10-3/4-ounce can cream of mushroom soup
1 10-3/4-ounce can cream of chicken soup
1/2 cup slivered, blanched almonds

Spread half of noodles over bottom of lightly greased, 13- x 9- x 2-in. baking pan. Top with half each of tuna, cheese, asparagus, mushrooms and water chestnuts. Repeat layers. Combine soups; spread over top of casserole. Sprinkle with almonds. Bake at 325º for 35 to 40 minutes, until heated through and beginning to brown on top. **Note:** Oven temperature may be increased to 350º near the end of baking time to brown casserole. Serves 20.

—Alice E. Peterson, Scarville, Iowa

TUNA-MACARONI DELIGHT

1-1/2 cups milk, warm
1/4 cup butter
1 cup macaroni, cooked, drained
3 eggs, beaten
1 cup soft bread crumbs
1/2 cup cheddar cheese, grated
1 tablespoon parsley, chopped
1 teaspoon onion, chopped
1 12-ounce can tuna fish, well drained

Heat together milk and butter; add to macaroni. Stir in beaten eggs; fold in remaining ingredients, adding tuna last. Turn into greased, 1-1/2-quart casserole or a greased mold. Bake at 325º for 50 minutes or until firm. Garnish with fresh parsley, if desired. —Mary Jo Altstaetter, Bellefontaine, Ohio

LOBSTER AND RIGATONI CASSEROLE

2 tablespoons butter, melted
4 ounces mushrooms, sliced
1/4 cup parsley, chopped
1 teaspoon dry mustard
1/2 teaspoon salt
Dash freshly ground pepper

1 5-1/2-ounce can lobster,
  drained
1 cup sour cream
4 cups rigatoni noodles, cooked,
  drained
1/2 cup Parmesan cheese, grated

In melted butter saute mushrooms for 5 minutes. Add parsley, mustard, salt and pepper. Break lobster into small pieces, discarding bony tissue. Add lobster and sour cream to mushroom mixture. Mix lightly; heat thoroughly. Place rigatoni into greased casserole or 4 to 6 individual casseroles; pour mushroom-lobster mixture over top. Sprinkle with cheese. Broil 3 to 4 inches from heat, until cheese is melted and brown. Serves 4 to 6.

—Mrs. Dale Engelman, Jansen, Nebraska

RING OF PLENTY

2 cups milk, hot
1/4 cup butter
2 cups American cheese,
  shredded
2 eggs, well beaten
2 cups soft bread crumbs

2 tablespoons each minced
  parsley, minced onion,
  chopped pimento
1 teaspoon salt
1/4 teaspoon pepper
8 ounces macaroni, cooked,
  drained

Combine milk and butter. Blend in cheese and eggs. Add bread crumbs, parsley, onion, pimento, salt and pepper. Stir in cooked noodles. Pour into well-greased, 10-in. ring mold or other baking dish. Set in pan filled 1 in. deep with water; bake at 350° for 30 minutes or until set. Unmold onto hot platter; fill center with creamed seafood, chicken or vegetable, if desired. Serves 8. **Note:** To make a Casserole of Plenty, use half of all ingredients. Bake in a 1-1/2-quart casserole.—**Cora May Gearhart, Three Rivers, Michigan**

PASTA

3 to 3-1/2 cups flour, divided
2 eggs

1/2 cup water
1/2 teaspoon salt

In large bowl thoroughly combine 2 cups flour, eggs, water and salt. Gradually add flour to form a stiff dough. Knead about 5 minutes. Form into ball. Cover; let stand 10 minutes. Divide into quarters. Roll out one section at a time until very thin. Allow dough to dry slightly. Cut into strips of any width desired. Cook in rapidly boiling, salted water. **Note:** To make egg noodles, use 3 eggs rather than 2 in above recipe. Also, substitute 4 egg yolks for water. To make green noodles, liquefy 10 ounces frozen, chopped spinach in electric blender. Strain. Follow above recipe, but substitute strained spinach for 1/2 cup water.   —**Country Woman staff**

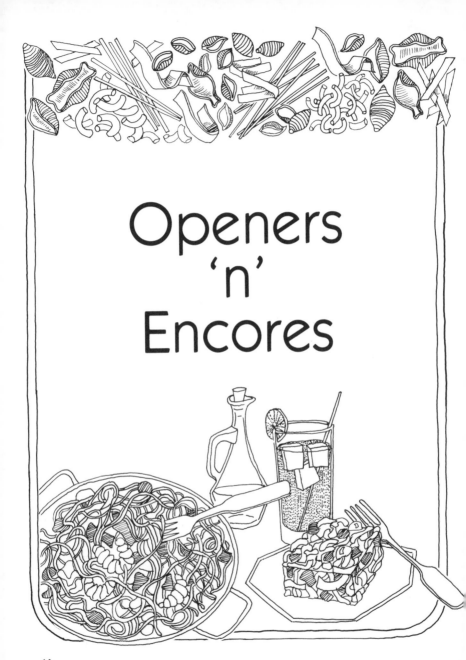

Openers 'n' Encores

Garden Crispers

SUMMER MACARONI SALAD

Salad:
16 ounces macaroni, cooked, drained, cooled
1 green pepper, chopped
3 carrots, grated
1 onion, chopped

Sauce:
1 cup white vinegar
3/4 cup sugar
2 cups mayonnaise
1 14-ounce can sweetened condensed milk
Pinch salt

Salad: Combine macaroni, green pepper, carrots and onion. **Sauce:** Blend together vinegar, sugar, mayonnaise, milk and salt. Add to cooked macaroni and raw vegetable mixture. Chill overnight. **Note:** Salad keeps well in the refrigerator for several days. —**Dawn Lorenz, Gladbrook, Iowa**

RIGATONI-SALMON SALAD

8 ounces rigatoni noodles
1 teaspoon plus 3 tablespoons olive oil, divided
8 ounces French-cut green beans
1 16-ounce can salmon, drained, flaked, reserving juice
1 tablespoon liquid from salmon
3 tablespoons wine vinegar
1/2 teaspoon basil
1/2 teaspoon garlic salt
1/2 cup green onion, chopped
3 tablespoons parsley, chopped
Salt and pepper to taste
1/4 cup Parmesan cheese, grated
2 fresh tomatoes, chopped

Cook rigatoni in 3 quarts salted water to which 1 teaspoon olive oil has been added. Drain; rinse with cold water. Cook beans until tender-crisp. Drain; plunge into cold water. Drain again. Combine rigatoni and beans. Blend together 1 tablespoon salmon liquid, 3 tablespoons olive oil, vinegar, basil and garlic salt. Toss into rigatoni and beans. Gently fold in salmon, onion and parsley. Salt and pepper to taste. Just before serving, toss with Parmesan and tomatoes. —**Mrs. Morey Wadleigh, Herscher, Illinois**

TASTY MACARONI SALAD

8 ounces shell macaroni, cooked drained, cooled
1/2 cup green onion, chopped
1 large bell pepper, chopped
2 pimentos, chopped
1/2 cup celery, chopped
3 hard-cooked eggs, chopped
1 large dill pickle, chopped
Salt to taste
1/2 to 3/4 cup mayonnaise

Combine ingredients in order listed. Refrigerate several hours to allow flavors to blend. Serves 8. —**Shirley Clinkscales, Anguilla, Mississippi**

SPAGHETTI SALAD

Salad:

1 cup spaghetti, broken into 2-in. pieces, cooked, drained, cooled
1 small head cabbage, grated
1 cup celery, finely diced
3/4 cup onion, minced

1 2-ounce jar pimento, chopped
1/2 cup green pepper, finely chopped
6 hard-cooked eggs, chopped, divided

Dressing:

3/4 cup prepared coleslaw dressing
1/2 cup mayonnaise
1 teaspoon salt

1 teaspoon coarse ground pepper
Paprika for garnish

Salad: To spaghetti add cabbage, celery, onion, pimento, green pepper and egg, reserving some egg for garnish. **Dressing:** Combine coleslaw dressing, mayonnaise, salt and pepper; add to spaghetti mixture. Mix just until all is moistened. Garnish with egg and paprika. **Note:** More or less mayonnaise may be used, depending on amount of cabbage.

—**Marthabelle Keim, Salisbury, Pennsylvania**

Noodle Notables

MACARONI AND CHEESE SALAD

Salad:

3 cups ham, cooked, cubed
3/4 cup macaroni, cooked, drained
8 ounces Swiss cheese, cubed
2 medium stalks celery, chopped

2 tomatoes, cubed
1 tablespoon parsley, chopped
1/2 teaspoon salt
Dash pepper

Dressing:

1/3 cup oil, divided
3 ounces bleu cheese, softened
1/2 teaspoon salt
1/8 teaspoon pepper

1/8 teaspoon garlic, minced
1 cup dairy sour cream
3 tablespoons cider vinegar

Salad: In large bowl thoroughly combine all ingredients. Chill. **Dressing:** Gradually add 2 tablespoons oil to softened cheese; blend at low speed until smooth. Add remaining oil, seasonings, sour cream and vinegar, one ingredient at a time, blending until smooth after each. Cover; chill. Mix well before using. Just before serving, fold 1/2 cup dressing into salad. Serve atop lettuce leaves. Garnish with crumbled bleu cheese, if desired. **Note:** Dressing recipe makes about 2 cups, but salad only requires 1/2 cup.

—**Norma Lee Harkins, Greenville, Michigan**

TURKEY-WALNUT SALAD

1 cup shell macaroni, cooked, drained, cooled
2 cups turkey, cooked, cubed, cooled
1 cup pineapple tidbits, drained
1/4 cup green pepper, chopped
3/4 cup black walnuts, chopped, divided
1 cup salad dressing
1 teaspoon black walnut flavoring (Tone's)

Thoroughly combine macaroni, turkey, pineapple, green pepper and 1/2 cup black walnuts. Mix salad dressing and black walnut flavoring. Stir 1/2 cup of dressing into macaroni mixture. Serve on lettuce-lined plates, garnished with more black walnuts. **Note:** Extra dressing, as is or sweetened with honey, may be used in mixed-fruit salads.
—Donna DeBower
Allison, Iowa

MACARONI SALAD

16 ounces spiral noodles, cooked, drained, cooled
4 cups celery, chopped
2 dozen hard-cooked eggs
1 10-ounce package frozen peas, cooked, drained, cooled
2 16-ounce cans pineapple tidbits, drained
1 4-ounce jar pimento
1 large onion, chopped
3 tablespoons salt
2 tablespoons sugar
2 tablespoons dry mustard
4 to 5 cups cashew nuts, chopped
1 quart salad dressing

Toss together all ingredients, thinning salad dressing with pineapple juice, if desired. **Note:** Salad keeps for several days refrigerated.
—Christeen K. Urish, Freeport, Illinois

MANDARIN CHICKEN SALAD

2 cups chicken, cooked, cubed
1 tablespoon onion, chopped
1 teaspoon salt
1 cup fresh, seedless grapes
1 cup celery, diced
1 cup mandarin oranges, drained, divided
1/3 cup slivered almonds, optional
1 cup ring OR shell macaroni, cooked, drained, cooled
1 cup salad dressing
1 cup whipped cream, unsweetened
Paprika for garnish

Combine chicken, onion and salt. Refrigerate several hours. Blend in grapes, celery, 3/4 cup mandarin oranges, slivered almonds, macaroni and salad dressing. Refrigerate until ready to serve. Just before serving, fold in whipped cream. Garnish with mandarin oranges and paprika. Serves 12.
—Julie Ellingson, Hanley Falls, Minnesota

WHEELER SALAD

Salad:

3 cups ring macaroni, cooked, drained, cooled
3 cups chicken, cooked, cubed, cooled
1 medium cucumber, chopped
2 medium carrots, grated
1 cup celery, diced
2 tomatoes, diced
1/4 cup onion, finely chopped
3 tablespoons green pepper, chopped
4 radishes, sliced
1 cup pineapple tidbits, drained
1 cup red grapes, halved and seeded OR green grapes, halved

Dressing:

1 cup salad dressing
1/2 cup cream
2 tablespoons vinegar
2 tablespoons sugar
1/2 teasoon onion salt
Salt and pepper to taste

Salad: Combine all ingredients. **Dressing:** Blend all ingredients. Fold dressing into salad. **—Thelma Meyer, Petersburg, North Dakota**

GERMAN MACARONI SALAD

5 slices bacon
1/2 cup sugar
3 tablespoons flour
1/2 teaspoon salt
1/8 teaspoon pepper
1/3 cup vinegar
1 4-ounce can mushroom pieces, drained, reserving liquid
Mushroom liquid plus enough water to make 1 cup
1 cup shell macaroni, uncooked
1/2 cup onion, chopped
1/2 cup celery, chopped

Fry bacon until crisp; drain, reserving drippings. Crumble bacon; set aside. Combine sugar, flour, salt and pepper; blend into bacon drippings. Combine vinegar and mushroom liquid plus water. Add to flour mixture; cook until thickened. Meanwhile, cook noodles; drain. To steaming noodles add hot, thickened dressing. Add mushrooms, bacon, onion and celery; toss to coat pasta evenly. Serve warm. **—Lynda Loeffler, Stanford, Illinois**

OVERNIGHT PASTA SALAD

2 cups lettuce, shredded
Salt and pepper to taste
4 ounces tiny shell macaroni, cooked, drained, cooled
2 hard-cooked eggs, sliced
1 cup ham, cooked, cut into Julienne strips
1 cup frozen peas, thawed
1/2 cup Swiss cheese, shredded
1/2 cup mayonnaise OR salad dressing
1/4 cup dairy sour cream
1 tablespoon green onion, chopped
1 teaspoon prepared mustard
Paprika and snipped parsley, optional

Place lettuce in bottom of 2-quart casserole. Sprinkle with salt and pepper. Top with cooled macaroni. Place a layer of egg slices on top; salt lightly. Next, make a layer of ham strips, then peas, then shredded cheese. Combine mayonnaise, sour cream, green onion and mustard. Spread over top of salad, sealing to edge of dish. Cover; refrigerate 24 hours. Sprinkle with paprika and snipped parsley, if desired. Toss before serving. Serves 4.

—Mrs. A.J. Ballas, Crown Point, Indiana

YUMMY MACARONI SALAD

Salad:

3 cups macaroni, cooked, drained, cooled
2 4-ounce packages dried beef, torn into small pieces
1/4 cup parsley, chopped
2 cups celery, diagonally cut
1/2 cup sweet pickle relish

2 tablespoons onion, chopped
1 4-ounce jar pimento OR 1/2 cup sweet red pepper, diced
4 hard-cooked eggs, chopped, divided
Olives and paprika for garnish

Dressing:

1 cup salad dressing
1 cup dairy sour cream
1/3 cup milk

1/3 cup lemon juice
2 tablespoons sweet pickle juice
1 teaspoon prepared mustard

Salad: Combine macaroni, dried beef, parsley, celery, relish, onion, pimento and half of eggs. Reserve remaining eggs plus olives and paprika for garnish. **Dressing:** Combine all ingredients; fold into macaroni mixture. Top with remaining eggs, olives and paprika.

—Bertha Traver, Ryan, Iowa

CRAB SALAD ROLOFF

1/2 cup green pepper, finely chopped
1 cup celery, finely chopped
1 cup onion, minced
2 tablespoons butter
3 cups tiny shell macaroni, cooked, drained
1 4-1/4-ounce can small crab meat, drained
1 4-1/2-ounce can small shrimp, drained

4 hard-cooked eggs, chopped
1 cup salad dressing
Salt and pepper to taste
1 10-3/4-ounce can cream of celery soup
1 10-3/4-ounce can cream of mushroom soup
Crushed potato chips for topping

Saute green pepper, celery and onion in butter until vegetables are tender. Add to cooked macaroni. Blend in crab meat, shrimp, eggs, salad dressing, salt, pepper and soups. Place into casserole dish; top with crushed potato chips. Bake for 20 to 30 minutes at 325°. **Note:** Salad may be prepared in advance, refrigerated overnight, and baked for 1 hour the following day.

—Mrs. William Duncan, Tekoa, Washington

COLD MACARONI AND SHRIMP SALAD

Salad:
2 cups shell macaroni, cooked, drained, cooled
1/2 cup cheese, shredded
1 cup celery, chopped
1/4 cup onion, minced
5 hard-cooked eggs, chopped
1 cup peas, cooked
1 4-1/2-ounce can shrimp, drained

Dressing:
1 cup salad dressing
1/2 cup cream
2 tablespoons sugar
1/2 teaspoon pepper
1 tablespoon prepared mustard
1/2 teaspoon celery salt, optional
1 teaspoon salt

Salad: Combine cold macaroni and remaining ingredients EXCEPT peas and shrimp. **Dressing:** Combine all ingredients thoroughly. Gradually stir dressing into macaroni mixture. Gently fold in peas and shrimp so as not to crush. Refrigerate; serve cold. **—Barbara Johnson, Lakota, North Dakota**

SEA SHELL SALAD

Salad:
2 cups shell macaroni, cooked, drained, cooled

1 11-ounce can mandarin oranges, drained
1 4-1/2-ounce can shrimp, drained

Dressing:
1/4 cup salad dressing
1/4 cup dairy sour cream
1 tablespoon sweet pickle relish
2 tablespoons chili sauce

1/2 teaspoon salt
Dash pepper
1/2 cup celery, chopped
1 tablespoon onion, minced

Salad: Combine macaroni, oranges and shrimp. **Dressing:** Combine all ingredients; fold into macaroni mixture. Chill; serve on lettuce with crackers. Serves 6. **—Mrs. Ralph Pierce, Oakland, Iowa**

Refreshing Finales

GERMAN SWEET NOODLES

10 ounces narrow noodles, cooked, drained
2 eggs, beaten
1/2 to 1 cup sugar

1 5-1/3-ounce can evaporated milk OR sweet cream
Cinnamon to taste

Place cooked, drained noodles into greased, 9-in. square baking pan. Combine beaten eggs, sugar to taste and milk or cream; pour over noodles. (Egg mixture should be just enough to barely cover noodles.) Sprinkle with cinnamon; bake at 350º for 35 minutes or until set. Cut into squares; serve hot.
—Carla Voran, Kingman, Kansas

NOODLES ALMANDINE

8 ounces broad noodles, cooked, drained
2 tablespoons sour cream
1 tablespoon lemon rind, grated
1 tablespoon orange rind, grated
1 heaping tablespoon sugar
1/2 cup toasted almonds
1/3 cup white raisins, plumped in hot water
1 tablespoon sugared cinnamon

Separate drained noodles with a fork. Add sour cream, grated lemon and orange rinds, sugar, toasted almonds and raisins. Blend thoroughly with wooden spoon, being careful not to mash noodles. Turn into serving bowl. Sprinkle with sugared cinnamon; serve immediately. **Note:** Recipe may also be baked, but 2 beaten egg yolks, 2 tablespoons fine bread crumbs and 2 beaten egg whites must be added. Bake in greased pan for 25 to 30 minutes at 350°.　**—Victoria L. Rinelli, Wauwatosa, Wisconsin**

NOODLE PUDDING

16 ounces wide egg noodles, cooked, drained
1/2 cup sour cream
1/2 cup cottage cheese
1/2 cup cream cheese
1 cup sugar
1 teaspoon cinnamon
1-1/2 teaspoons salt
1-1/2 teaspoons vanilla
4 eggs, beaten
1 20-ounce can crushed pineapple, drained
1/2 cup raisins
1/2 cup butter
1 cup milk

Thoroughly combine all ingredients EXCEPT butter and milk. Coat bottom and sides of 13- x 9-in. baking pan with melted butter, pouring excess butter into noodle mixture. Place noodle mixture into baking pan. Pour milk over top. Bake at 350° for 1 hour.　**—Roxanne Cohen, Dexter, Maine**

CINNAMON KUGEL

8 ounces broad egg noodles, cooked, drained
3 large eggs, slightly beaten
8 ounces creamed cottage cheese
1/2 cup dairy sour cream
2 tablespoons butter, melted
1/3 cup sugar
3/4 teaspoon salt
1/2 teaspoon grated lemon rind
2 teaspoons ground cinnamon
1/8 teaspoon ground nutmeg
3/4 cup golden raisins
1/3 cup buttered cornflake crumbs

Place cooked, drained noodles in large mixing bowl. Combine eggs, cottage cheese, sour cream, 2 tablespoons butter, sugar, salt, lemon rind, cinnamon and nutmeg. Mix gently; add to noodles. Stir in raisins. Place in 2-quart baking dish. Sprinkle buttered crumbs over noodles. Bake at 375° for 20 minutes. Serve with additional sour cream, if desired.

—Florence Lorence, Racine, Wisconsin

ITALIAN NOODLE SQUARES

8 ounces very thin egg noodles, cooked, drained
6 eggs, slightly beaten
3/4 cup milk
12 ounces ricotta cheese
2 tablespoons orange juice
1/2 cup sugar
1 tablespoon vanilla
Powdered sugar, optional

Combine all ingredients except powdered sugar; pour into greased, 9- x 9- x 2-in. or slightly larger baking pan. Bake at 350º for 1 hour or until golden brown. Cut into squares; serve hot or cold. Sprinkle with powdered sugar, if desired. **—Marie Pontillo, Bridgeport, Connecticut**

NOODLE-PUDDING SQUARES

4 eggs, beaten
1/2 cup sugar
1/2 cup butter
3/4 pint sour cream
1 20-ounce can crushed pineapple, drained
6 ounces broad noodles, cooked, drained, cooled
1 tablespoon sugared cinnamon
Maraschino cherries for garnish

Combine eggs, sugar, butter, sour cream and pineapple. Blend in noodles. Pour mixture into greased baking dish. Sprinkle with sugared cinnamon; garnish with maraschino cherries. Bake at 350º for 45 minutes. Serve warm or cooled, cut into squares. **Note:** Noodle-pudding squares freeze well.

—Lois Wharam, Carlisle, Pennsylvania

ACINI DE PEPE SALAD

1 cup (1/2 box) Acini de Pepe soupmacs, uncooked
1 cup sugar
2 tablespoons flour
1/2 teaspoon salt
3 egg yolks, beaten
1 15-ounce can pineapple tidbits, drained, reserving juice
1 15-1/4-ounce can crushed pineapple, drained, reserving juice
2 11-ounce cans mandarin oranges, drained
1 10-1/2-ounce bag miniature marshmallows
4 cups sweetened whipped cream OR 2 packages prepared Dream Whip
1 cup chopped nuts, optional

Cook soupmacs until well done, 30 to 40 minutes. Blanch, drain and cool. In medium-sized saucepan combine sugar, flour, salt, egg yolks and 1-3/4 cups pineapple juice. Cook over medium heat until thick; cool. Thoroughly combine sauce and cooked soupmacs in 8-quart bowl. Cover; chill overnight. Just before serving add pineapple, mandarin oranges, miniature marshmallows and whipped cream or Dream Whip. Add nuts, if desired. Serves 20. **—Debbie Maas, Cheyenne, Wyoming**

SPECIAL SPEZZIELLO SALAD

1 cup Spezziello soupmacs OR
  ring macaroni, cooked, drained
1 cup powdered sugar
1/4 cup lemon juice
2 eggs, well beaten
1 cup crushed pineapple, drained

1 package whipped topping mix
1/2 cup half-and-half cream, cold
1/2 teaspoon vanilla
1 cup miniature marshmallows
4 tart apples, peeled, diced

Place cooked, drained noodles into a bowl. In a saucepan combine powdered sugar, lemon juice and eggs. Cook, stirring, until thick. Pour over cooked pasta. Stir in pineapple. Let set covered in refrigerator overnight. Next day, combine topping mix, half-and-half cream and vanilla, following package directions. Fold into noodle mixture, along with marshmallows and apple pieces. **—Durelle Zacharias, Persia, Iowa**

FRUITED MACARONI SALAD

10 ounces ring macaroni, uncooked
2 cups crushed pineapple, well
  drained, reserving juice
2 cups chunky-style mixed fruit,
  well drained, reserving juice
1 cup mandarin oranges, well
  drained, reserving juice
1/2 cup sugar

2 tablespoons flour
2 eggs, beaten
1 3-ounce box lemon gelatin
1 10-1/2-ounce bag miniature
  marshmallows
1 cup chopped pecans, optional
2 cups whipped topping OR
  1/2 pint heavy cream, whipped

Cook macaroni as directed on package, but omit the salt. Chill. Combine juices from fruits with sugar, flour and eggs; cook until thickened. Add dry lemon gelatin; chill. Combine pineapple, mixed fruit, oranges and marshmallows. Stir in chilled gelatin mixture. Fold in nuts and cooked, cooled macaroni. Refrigerate 24 hours. Just before serving, fold in whipped topping or cream. **—Lela Giefer, Parsons, Kansas**

EVERLASTING MICROWAVE SALAD

1/2 cup sugar
1 tablespoon flour
1/4 cup lemon juice
2 eggs, slightly beaten
2 apples, cubed

1 8-1/2-ounce can crushed
  pineapple, drained
1 cup shell macaroni, cooked,
  drained
1 cup whipping cream, whipped

In 1-quart glass measure combine sugar, flour, lemon juice and eggs. Microwave on ROAST (70% Power) for 3-1/2 minutes or until thick, stirring once during cooking. In 2-quart serving dish combine apples, pineapple and cooked macaroni. Stir in sauce; chill. At serving time fold whipped cream into salad. Serves 4. **—Karen Ver Meer, Pella, Iowa**

PASTA FRUIT FLUFF

2 cups durum shell OR elbow macaroni, cooked, drained, cooled
1 11-ounce can mandarin orange slices, drained
1 20-ounce can pineapple chunks, drained
1 cup maraschino cherries, drained
1 cup dairy sour cream
3/4 cup sugar
1/2 cup coconut, shredded OR walnuts, chopped

In large bowl combine cooled macaroni, fruits, sour cream and sugar; mix thoroughly. Sprinkle with coconut or walnuts.

—Mrs. Marian Seuferling, Louisburg, Kansas

APPLE-NOODLE DESSERT

1-1/2 cups apples, sliced
2 cups thin noodles, uncooked
1 cup water
1/4 cup nuts, chopped
1/4 cup currants OR raisins
1/2 teaspoon cinnamon
1/2 cup brown sugar
1 tablespoon lemon juice
1/2 teaspoon salt
1 tablespoon butter, melted
Whipped cream for topping

Arrange apple slices in greased, 1-1/2-quart casserole. Bake covered at 375⁰ for 15 minutes. Meanwhile, cook noodles; spread cooked, drained noodles over apples. Combine remaining ingredients EXCEPT whipped cream; pour nut mixture over noodles. Return to oven; bake uncovered 15 minutes. Serve with a dollop of whipped cream. Serves 4.
**—Nancy Hill
Edgewood, New Mexico**

RING O' SALAD

1 3-1/8-ounce box lemon pudding mix
7 ounces ring macaroni, cooked, drained, cooled
1 20-ounce can crushed pineapple, well drained
1 15-1/2-ounce can fruit cocktail, well drained
1 cup miniature marshmallows
1 apple, chopped
1 cup grapes, halved, optional
4 ounces purchased whipped topping

Cook lemon pudding according to package directions. Chill well. Add macaroni, pineapple, fruit cocktail and miniature marshmallows to cooled pudding. Refrigerate overnight. Just before serving, fold in apple pieces, grapes and whipped topping. Serves 12.
**—Leona Wessels
Huron, South Dakota**

Stovetop
Specialties

Little Extras

POLISH NOODLES AND CABBAGE

1/2 cup onion, chopped
1/4 cup butter, melted
    4 cups cabbage, chopped
1/2 teaspoon salt

1/8 teaspoon pepper
8 ounces egg noodles, cooked,
   drained
1/2 cup sour cream

In large skillet saute onion in butter until soft. Add cabbage; saute until cabbage is tender-crisp, about 5 minutes. Sprinkle with salt and pepper. Stir hot noodles into cabbage; add sour cream. Cook 5 minutes longer, stirring frequently. Serves 6. **—Nancy Robaidek, Krakow, Wisconsin**

FRIED MACARONI

2 cups elbow macaroni
2 quarts water

2 or 3 tablespoons butter
Salt and pepper to taste

Cook macaroni in 2 quarts water with no salt added. Drain thoroughly. Melt butter over medium heat in heavy skillet. Add cooked, drained macaroni. Fry as you would potatoes, turning as macaroni browns. Salt and pepper to taste. Serve in place of potatoes. **—Rose Kean, Grand Meadow, Minnesota**

POLISH PASTA

1 cup flour
1 cup mashed potatoes

1 egg

Thoroughly combine flour, potatoes and egg. Sprinkle with salt and pepper if using unseasoned mashed potatoes. Drop by scant tablespoonfuls into boiling water. Cook until no longer doughy. Serve hot with your favorite sauce or gravy. **—Margaret Bittner, Germansville, Pennsylvania**

SPAGHETTI OMELET

    4 eggs
    1 small onion, minced
1/4 cup Parmesan cheese, grated
    8 ounces whole wheat spaghetti,
    cooked, drained

1/4 cup butter
2 tablespoons toasted sunflower
   seeds

Beat together eggs, onion and cheese. Add spaghetti; mix well. Heat butter in 10- or 12-in. skillet; add spaghetti mixture. Sprinkle with sunflower seeds. Cook over medium heat until firm and well browned on bottom. Turn to brown other side. Serves 4.
—Anna-Margaret Binder, Port Allegany, Pennsylvania

CLAM SAUCE SPAGHETTI

1 small onion, chopped
2 tablespoons butter
2 cloves garlic, chopped
1 10-ounce can clams, drained, reserving liquid
1 cup clam juice
1 2-ounce can red peppers, diced
2 tablespoons parsley, chopped
1 teaspoon oregano
Salt and pepper to taste
1/2 cup cornstarch
Water as needed
1/2 cup heavy cream
8 ounces spaghetti, cooked, drained

Saute onion in melted butter over low heat. When onion is golden, add garlic. Cook 1 minute. Add clams and clam juice. Stir in peppers, parsley and seasonings. Combine cornstarch and enough water to make a paste. Thicken cream with cornstarch mixture; stir into skillet. Blend in pasta; serve immediately. **—Mrs. Paul Zylstra, Duvall, Washington**

VERMICELLI 'N' ZUCCHINI

2 medium zucchini
1 small onion, chopped
1/4 cup olive oil
2 cups fresh OR canned tomato, peeled, chopped
2 cups water
2 tablespoons chopped, fresh basil OR 1 teaspoon dried
8 ounces vermicelli, cut into 1-in. pieces
Salt and pepper to taste

Wash zucchini; scrape lightly with a knife. Cut into 1-in. cubes. Saute onion in oil until light brown. Add tomato; simmer 5 minutes. Pour in water; bring to boil. Add zucchini and basil; cook 5 minutes. Stir in vermicelli; cook over low heat until pasta is tender, about 15 minutes, stirring occasionally. Season with salt and pepper; serve hot. Serves 4.
—Annette M. Morra, Carmel, New York

PASTA PATE

8 ounces cream cheese, softened
1/4 cup cheddar cheese, grated
1/2 cup dairy sour cream
3 tablespoons onion, finely chopped
3 tablespoons green pepper, finely chopped
2 tablespoons pimento, chopped
1/4 teaspoon cayenne pepper
1 cup egg noodles OR novelty noodles, cooked, drained, cooled

In mixing bowl blend all ingredients EXCEPT pasta. Gently fold cooled pasta into cheese mixture. Place into lightly greased, 6- x 5- x 2-in. loaf pan. Cover; chill until firm, at least 1 hour. Unmold onto cheeseboard or small serving platter. Serve with pumpernickel or onion-flavored crackers. Serves 8.
—Rochelle SeeWald, Prior Lake, Minnesota

MOM'S SPAGHETTI SAUCE AND MEATBALLS

Sauce:

1 large onion, chopped
1/8 teaspoon garlic salt
2 tablespoons oil
2 28-ounce cans tomatoes
1 cup water
1 teaspoon dried basil
1/2 cup parsley, chopped

1 tablespoon Italian herb
  seasoning
2-1/2 teaspoons salt
1/2 teaspoon pepper
1 15-ounce can tomato sauce
2 6-ounce cans tomato paste

Meatballs:

3 to 4 pounds ground beef
2 teaspoons salt
1 cup dry bread crumbs, fine
1/2 teaspoon pepper
1/4 cup parsley, chopped

1/8 teaspoon garlic salt
3/4 cup Parmesan cheese, grated
3 eggs
1/2 cup evaporated milk
2 onions, minced

Sauce: In large saucepan saute onion and garlic salt in oil until onion is transparent. Add tomatoes; bring to boil. Simmer uncovered for 20 minutes. Add remaining ingredients; simmer uncovered 2 hours more, stirring occasionally. **Meatballs:** Thoroughly combine all ingredients. Add a little more milk or some water if mixture seems dry. Shape into medium-sized balls. Place into large, shallow pan; brown in 375° oven for 15 minutes. Add meatballs to simmering sauce; cook while preparing 32 ounces spaghetti. Serves 10.   **—Sara Tatham, Plymouth, New Hampshire**

SPICY, SAUCY MEATBALLS

Meatballs:

3 slices bread
2 eggs, well beaten
1 pound ground beef OR venison
1/2 teaspoon basil
1/2 teaspoon garlic salt

1/4 teaspoon nutmeg
2 teaspoons salt
1 teaspoon pepper
1/4 cup Parmesan cheese, grated

Sauce:

3 8-ounce cans tomato sauce
1 6-ounce can tomato paste
3 tomato paste cans water
1 teaspoon basil
1/2 teaspoon garlic salt

1/4 teaspoon nutmeg
2 tablespoons sugar
1 teaspoon salt
1/2 teaspoon pepper

Meatballs: Soak bread in eggs until bread is thoroughly moistened. Combine all ingredients, including eggs not soaked up by bread. Form into balls. **Sauce:** Combine all ingredients; bring to a boil. Drop meatballs into sauce. Simmer 1-1/2 to 2 hours, until meatballs are done and sauce is thick.

—Janet Fesenmyer, Marble, Pennsylvania

Twirlers and Fillers

PASTA WITH STIR-FRIED CHICKEN

2 tablespoons butter
2 tablespoons flour
1/4 teaspoon cracked pepper
2 teaspoons salt, divided
2 cups milk
1 cube chicken bouillon
1/4 cup Parmesan cheese, grated
24 ounces asparagus, cut into
  2-in. pieces
8 ounces mushrooms, thinly sliced
1 medium carrot, thinly sliced

1 medium zucchini, halved length-
  wise, cut into 1/4-in. slices
3 green onions, cut into 3-in.
  pieces
1/4 cup plus 2 tablespoons olive OR
  salad oil, divided
4 chicken breasts, cut into thin
  strips
1/2 cup frozen peas
16 ounces spaghetti, cooked,
  drained

Melt butter in 2-quart saucepan over medium heat; stir in flour, pepper and
1/4 teaspoon salt. Gradually stir in milk; add bouillon. Cook, stirring constantly, until sauce is slightly thickened and smooth. Remove from heat; stir
in cheese until melted. Keep sauce warm. Using 8-quart Dutch oven, saute
asparagus, mushrooms, carrot, zucchini and green onions in 1/4 cup hot oil
seasoned with 3/4 teaspoon salt. Cook, stirring frequently, over medium-
high heat until vegetables are tender-crisp, about 5 minutes. With slotted
spoon remove vegetables to bowl; set aside. Using same Dutch oven, add 2
more tablespoons oil and 1 teaspoon salt. Cook chicken in Dutch oven over
medium-high heat, stirring frequently, until chicken is tender, about 5 minutes. Return vegetables to Dutch oven; add peas. Cook until vegetables are
heated through, about 5 minutes, stirring occasionally. Add sauce and
vegetable mixture to hot spaghetti; mix well. Serves 8.   **—Mrs. Henry Bruha**
Arcadia, Nebraska

SPAGHETTI ALLA CARBONARA

1/4 pound bacon, diced
1 medium onion, chopped
1 tablespoon butter
1/3 cup white wine
16 ounces spaghetti, cooked,
  drained

3 eggs, lightly beaten
2 tablespoons parsley, chopped
6 ounces Parmesan cheese,
  grated, divided
1/4 teaspoon pepper

Fry diced bacon and chopped onion in butter. Add wine; simmer slowly.
While cooking spaghetti, combine eggs, parsley, 4 ounces cheese and pepper; add to cooked, drained spaghetti. Pour hot bacon mixture over
spaghetti; stir well. Serve immediately, topped with remaining 2 ounces
cheese. Serves 4.   **—Joan E. Wagner, Mount Victory, Ohio**

ITALIAN MINESTRA ALLA GENOVESE

8 ounces fresh string beans OR
1 9-ounce package frozen,
French-cut beans
4 potatoes, peeled, sliced
3 tomatoes, peeled, sliced
2-1/2 quarts water
8 ounces Italian, long spaghetti,
uncooked

1 tablespoon salt
1/2 teaspoon pepper
1 clove garlic, crushed
1/2 teaspoon thyme
1/2 teaspoon basil
2 tablespoons tomato paste
3 tablespoons olive oil
1/2 cup Parmesan cheese, grated

Add string beans, potatoes and tomatoes to water in saucepan. Cook over medium heat for 15 minutes. Add spaghetti, salt and pepper. Cook 12 minutes longer or until spaghetti is tender. Meanwhile, in separate bowl, combine garlic, thyme, basil and tomato paste. Add olive oil, drop by drop, mixing steadily until smooth. Reduce heat beneath saucepan; VERY GRADUALLY add tomato paste mixture to noodles, stirring constantly. When well blended and hot, serve topped with Parmesan. Serves 8.

—Sandi Pierson, Grafton, New Hampshire

KASE NOODLE (Cottage Cheese Dumplings)

Dough:
6 egg yolks
2 whole eggs
1/2 teaspoon salt

2 tablespoons water
2 cups flour OR as needed

Filling:
3 cups dry cottage cheese OR
creamed cottage cheese, well
drained
3 eggs

1/4 teaspoon salt
1/4 cup green onions with some
tops, chopped

Topping:
1/2 cup sour cream
1/2 cup broth reserved from
cooking pasta

3/4 cup bread cubes, browned
in butter

Dough: Combine all ingredients EXCEPT flour, mixing until well blended. Add enough flour to make a stiff dough. Let rest while mixing filling. **Filling:** Thoroughly combine cottage cheese, eggs, salt and onion. Roll dough to 1/16 in. thick; cut into 3-in. squares. In center of each place 1 tablespoon cheese filling. Bring all four corners to center; pinch edges together. Cook dumplings in 3 quarts boiling, salted water for 5 to 7 minutes or until all pillows are floating. Drain, reserving 1/2 cup broth. **Topping:** Combine sour cream and reserved broth. Spoon over dumplings. Garnish with bread cubes. —Dorothy Laubach, Obeene, Oklahoma

SPAGHETTI 'N' EGGS

8 ounces spaghetti
1/4 pound bacon, diced
1/4 cup oil
1 onion, thinly sliced
1/4 pound prosciutto OR boiled
   ham, cut into strips

1/2 cup whipped butter
1/2 cup chicken broth, warm
4 egg yolks, beaten
1/2 cup parsley, finely chopped
1 cup Parmesan cheese, grated

As spaghetti cooks, brown diced bacon lightly for 5 minutes. Drain off bacon fat; add 1/4 cup oil to bacon. Saute onion until soft in skillet with bacon. Stir in ham; add cooked spaghetti. Add whipped butter, stirring to coat spaghetti. Blend in chicken broth. **Important:** Remove pan from heat before next step. Add beaten egg yolks, stirring quickly to blend. (Hot spaghetti will cook yolks; if skillet is left on the burner, yolks will scramble.) Blend in parsley; sprinkle with 1 cup Parmesan. Toss well; serve immediately with more grated cheese and pepper on the side. Serves 4.

—Victoria L. Rinelli, Wauwatosa, Wisconsin

SOPA DE FIDELO

8 ounces vermicelli
2 tablespoons shortening
1 pound ground beef
1 teaspoon salt
1 teaspoon pepper
3 cloves garlic, minced
2 cups onion, chopped
2 cups celery, chopped

1 cup water
1/2 cup green pepper, diced
1 29-ounce can tomatoes
1-1/2 cups whole kernel corn
1 tablespoon chili powder
8 ounces American cheese,
   grated

In electric frying pan preheated to 300°, saute vermicelli in shortening until lightly browned. Add ground beef. Cook, stirring, until beef loses red color. Gently stir in remaining ingredients except cheese. Lower frying pan temperature to 200°. Simmer for 25 minutes, stirring occasionally. Top with cheese. Cook covered for 5 minutes to melt cheese. **—Golda Freund Lebo, Kansas**

GROWING PASTA: *Noodles increase in bulk by about 50% during cooking. Use dry pasta when measuring ingredients for all recipes in this cookbook.*

NO STICKING: *To prevent noodles from sticking, first drain in a colander. Rinse under cold water; drain again.*

CHICKEN 'N' SPAGHETTI

1 stewing chicken OR 3 pounds chicken parts
1/4 cup oil
1-1/2 quarts water, hot
1 tablespoon salt
2 cups celery, chopped
1/3 cup green onion, chopped
1/3 cup green pepper, chopped
1/2 cup pimento, diced
12 ounces spaghetti
1-1/2 cups sliced, ripe olives
2 cups cheddar cheese, shredded, divided

In large kettle brown chicken in hot oil. Add water and salt. Cover; cook slowly until meat is tender. Remove meat from bones; chill chicken in broth overnight. Remove fat from broth. Saute celery, onion and green pepper in 1/4 cup fat. Add cooked vegetables plus pimento to broth. Bring to a boil; add spaghetti. Return to boiling; simmer until noodles are tender. Stir in olives and 1-3/4 cups cheese. Sprinkle with remaining cheese.

—Janice Burwash, Eatonville, Washington

RAVIOLI

Sauce:
4 pork steaks, cut into bite-size pieces
1 onion, diced
1 cup celery, chopped
2 8-ounce cans tomato sauce
1/2 cup carrots, sliced
1 teaspoon oregano
2 4-ounce cans mushrooms, undrained
Salt and pepper to taste

Pasta:
2 cups flour
Pinch salt
2 eggs
4 tablespoons olive oil
Lukewarm water

Filling:
1 cup ground beef
1 cup ground pork
2 eggs
1 clove garlic, minced
1/2 cup Parmesan cheese, grated
Salt and pepper to taste

Sauce: Brown pork steak; drain. Add onion and celery. When vegetables are tender, add tomato sauce, carrots, oregano, mushrooms plus liquid and salt and pepper; simmer 1 hour. **Pasta:** Combine flour and salt; add eggs and olive oil to well in center. Blend ingredients; add enough lukewarm water to make stiff dough. Knead until smooth and slightly elastic. Cover; let rest 10 minutes. Roll to 1/16 in. thick. **Filling:** Cook ground beef and pork thoroughly; drain. Add eggs, garlic, cheese and salt and pepper; cook thoroughly. Place filling by teaspoonfuls onto half of pasta circle. Fold pasta over, pressing firmly around each mound. Cut between mounds. Let rest 15 minutes; simmer in salted water for 5 to 7 minutes or until ravioli rises to surface and is slightly clear. Drop individual ravioli pillows into simmering sauce. Serves 6.   —Sheri Lynn Gay, Fairfield, Washington

TORTALACCHI

Filling:
2 eggs, beaten
2 cups cheese, grated
2 cups cracker crumbs

2 cups milk
1 15-ounce can spinach, drained

Dough:
4 cups flour
4 eggs

Water

Filling: Combine beaten eggs, 1-3/4 cups cheese and 1-3/4 cups cracker crumbs; cook slowly, gradually adding milk and stirring. When filling is thickened and resembles cottage cheese, add chopped spinach and enough additional cheese and cracker crumbs so that filling will stay in mounds when spooned onto dough. **Dough:** Make well in center of flour. Add eggs; mix with fork. Sprinkle with a little water if needed to absorb all flour. Roll to 1/16-in. thick. Cut into 2-in. strips. Place small mounds of filling 1-1/2 to 2 in. apart on dough. Cut between mounds. Bring 2 edges of dough up around each mound to form a hat. Press all edges to seal well. Set on wooden board to dry, about 2 hours. Add tortalacchi to a large pot of boiling, salted water. Return to a full boil; test for doneness. Strain cooked tortalacchi in colander. Serve topped with spaghetti sauce OR melted butter and grated Parmesan. Serves 4. **—Victoria L. Rinelli Wauwatosa, Wisconsin**

Cream of the Crop

FETTUCINI ALLA CARBONARA

4 eggs
1/4 cup whipping cream
16 ounces fettucini noodles,
    cooked, drained (do not rinse)
1/4 cup butter

1/2 pound bacon, fried, crumbled
1 cup Parmesan cheese, grated
Few grinds pepper
1/4 cup parsley, snipped

Place eggs and whipping cream in a bowl. Do not beat together. Let stand at room temperature for 2 to 3 hours. Toss cooked pasta with butter to coat. Beat eggs and cream; fold into noodle mixture. Stir in bacon bits, cheese, pepper and parsley. Serves 6. **—Gail M. Schutz, White Hall, Illinois**

MACARONI 'N' COTTAGE CHEESE

8 ounces elbow macaroni, cooked,
    drained
4 tablespoons butter

8 ounces small curd cottage cheese
Fried bacon bits, optional

Coat hot macaroni with butter. Add cottage cheese; mix well. Toss in bacon bits, if desired. **Note:** Wide egg noodles may be substituted for elbow macaroni. **—Marie Pontillo, Bridgeport, Connecticut**

SAUCY BEEF ROLLS

1-1/2 pounds round steak
3 tablespoons butter, melted
1-1/2 cups bread crumbs
1/2 cup mild cheddar cheese, shredded
1-1/2 teaspoons salt, divided
1/8 teaspoon plus dash pepper, divided
1/4 cup plus 2 tablespoons butter, divided
1/4 cup green onion, chopped
1/3 cup green peppers, chopped
1 6-ounce can tomato paste
1-1/2 cups water
1/4 cup dark corn syrup
2 tablespoons cider vinegar
1 teaspoon dried oregano leaves
16 ounces Italian-style spaghetti

Cut round steak into slices about 4 x 2 x 1/2 in. Pound on both sides until very thin. Combine 3 tablespoons melted butter, bread crumbs, cheese, 1/2 teaspoon salt and dash pepper. Spoon 1 to 2 tablespoons of mixture onto each piece of meat. Roll up meat; secure with toothpicks. Heat 2 tablespoons butter in a skillet over moderately low heat. Increase temperature to medium-high. Add some of the beef rolls; brown on all sides. Remove browned rolls from skillet. Continue until all meat rolls are browned. Saute onions and peppers in same skillet, over moderately low heat. Blend in tomato paste. Gradually stir in water, mixing well. Blend in corn syrup, cider vinegar, oregano, 1 teaspoon salt and 1/8 teaspoon pepper. Add meat rolls. Cook covered for 1-1/2 hours, turning meat occasionally. Meanwhile, cook spaghetti. Add 1/4 cup butter to drained noodles. Arrange noodles on serving platter. Top with meat and sauce. **Note:** Sauce may be thinned with water if necessary. Serves 6. —Nancy Grevenstuk
Byron Center, Michigan

PASTA CON CHILIES VERDES

2 slices bacon
1/2 cup onion, chopped
1 pound ground beef
1 28-ounce can tomatoes
1/2 cup water
1/4 cup chili sauce
2 green chilies, diced OR 1 4-ounce can chopped green chilies
1 teaspoon salt
1 teaspoon sugar
1/2 cup green pepper, chopped
4 ounces noodles, uncooked
1/4 cup cheddar cheese, grated

Fry bacon until crisp, remove from skillet. Add onion to bacon drippings; saute until tender but not brown. Add ground beef. Brown; drain. In blender combine tomatoes, water, chili sauce, chilies, salt and sugar until smooth. Add to meat mixture. Stir in green pepper and uncooked noodles. Cook covered over low heat for 30 minutes or until noodles are tender, stirring frequently. Stir in crumbled bacon; top with cheddar cheese. Serve immediately after cheese has melted. Serves 4. —Nancy Hill
Edgewood, New Mexico

LINGUINE BOLOGNESE

6 slices bacon	1/4 teaspoon nutmeg
2 tablespoons butter	1/8 teaspoon pepper
1 cup onion, chopped	1-1/2 cups beef bouillon
1/2 cup celery, diced	1/4 cup tomato sauce
1/2 cup carrot, diced	1 cup dry white wine
1 pound lean ground beef	12 ounces linguine
1 teaspoon salt	1/4 cup light cream

In large skillet fry bacon until crisp. Remove bacon; set aside. Add butter, onion, celery and carrots to 1 tablespoon bacon drippings. Saute vegetables until tender-crisp, stirring constantly. Add beef; cook until red color disappears. Blend in salt, nutmeg and pepper. Add broth and tomato sauce; simmer covered for 20 minutes. Add wine; simmer covered 20 minutes more. Meanwhile, cook linguine. Stir cream into sauce; spoon sauce over cooked, drained pasta. Garnish with crumbled bacon. Serves 4.

—Florence Lorence, Racine, Wisconsin

MEXICAN LUNCHEON

2 pounds pork sausage	2 cups elbow macaroni, cooked, drained
1 cup onion, diced	2 tablespoons sugar
1 cup green pepper, diced	1 tablespoon chili powder
1 pint canned tomatoes	1 teaspoon salt
2 cups sour cream	1 4-ounce can green chilies, optional

Saute sausage, onion and green pepper in large skillet or Dutch oven. When sausage is browned, pour off drippings. Add tomatoes, sour cream, macaroni, sugar, chili power, salt and chilies. Cook covered over low heat for 10 minutes, then uncovered 10 minutes more. Serves 8.

—Freda Kay Campbell, Cataldo, Idaho

ALL-AT-ONCE SPAGHETTI

1 large onion, chopped	Pepper to taste
1 tablespoon corn oil	2 6-ounce cans tomato paste
1 pound ground beef	3 cups water
2 teaspoons salt	8 ounces spaghetti
1 tablespoon Italian seasoning	Parmesan cheese, grated

Saute onion in oil. Add ground beef; cook, stirring, until meat loses red color. Drain off fat. Add seasonings. Pour in tomato paste and water; bring to a boil. Break spaghetti in half; gradually stir spaghetti into sauce. Cook covered for 20 to 30 minutes over medium heat, stirring occasionally. Top with grated cheese to serve. **—Mary Beth Gibbs, Columbia, North Carolina**

NOODLES WITH PORK BALLS

Pork Balls:

1 cup soft bread crumbs	1 teaspoon salt
1/3 cup milk	1 teaspoon lemon juice
1 pound lean ground pork	1/8 teaspoon paprika
1 egg	1/8 teaspoon nutmeg
1/4 cup onion, chopped	1 tablespoon butter

Sauce:

1 tablespoon butter, melted	1/4 teaspoon dry mustard
1 tablespoon flour	1-1/2 cups milk

Noodles:

8 ounces egg noodles, uncooked	2 tablespoons butter, melted
	2 tablespoons parsley, snipped

Pork Balls: Combine bread crumbs and milk. Add remaining ingredients EXCEPT 1 tablespoon butter, mixing well. Shape into 18 to 20 meatballs. Brown in 1 tablespoon butter. Cook covered for 20 minutes over low heat. Remove from skillet; keep warm. **Sauce:** To melted butter in skillet add 1 additional tablespoon butter. Stir in flour and dry mustard. Blend thoroughly. Add milk. Cook, stirring constantly, until sauce is thickened. Return pork balls to skillet. Heat thoroughly. **Noodles:** Cook pasta as directed on package. Drain. Toss with 2 tablespoons melted butter and 2 tablespoons parsley. Serve pork balls and sauce over noodles. Serves 4.

—**Margaret Johnson, Wells, Minnesota**

WHITE CLAM SAUCE SPAGHETTI

1/4 cup butter	1 clove garlic, crushed
1/4 cup olive oil	1 tomato, peeled, chopped
1 cup green onions and tops, chopped	Salt and pepper to taste
1 tablespoon parsley, snipped	2 7-1/2-ounce cans chopped clams, drained, reserving juice
1/2 teaspoon oregano	16 ounces spaghetti
1/2 teaspoon basil	1/4 cup parmesan cheese, grated

Heat butter and olive oil in skillet. Remove 2 tablespoons for use later. In remaining butter and oil saute onions until tender-crisp. Add parsley, oregano, basil, garlic, tomato, salt, pepper and clam juice. Simmer 5 minutes. If sauce is too thin, add 2 teaspoons cornstarch dissolved in 1 teaspoon water. Simmer until sauce is thickened. Add clams. Keep sauce hot. Cook spaghetti according to package directions. Drain. Return spaghetti to kettle in which it was cooked. Add reserved 2 tablespoons butter and oil mixture. Add 1/4 cup Parmesan. Toss to coat noodles evenly. Blend in half the sauce. Pass remaining sauce separately when serving.

—**Corinne Rickabaugh, Shreve, Ohio**

SKILLET DINNER

1-1/2 pounds ground beef
1 tablespoon olive oil OR
cooking oil
1-1/2 cups onion, chopped
1-1/2 cups celery, chopped
1-1/2 cups ketchup
1 cup water
1 tablespoon Worcestershire
sauce
2 teaspoons salt
1/8 teaspoon pepper
1/2 teaspoon dry mustard
1 teaspoon oregano OR to taste
16 ounces novelty noodles,
cooked, drained
1 cup American cheese,
shredded
1/2 cup Parmesan cheese, grated
2 tablespoons parsley, chopped

Saute beef in oil until red color disappears. Add onion and celery; cook until onion is soft. Add ketchup, water, Worcestershire sauce, salt, pepper, mustard and oregano; mix well. Stir in cooked, drained noodles; cover. Simmer to cook meat and blend flavors, 20 to 25 minutes. Just before serving, fold in American cheese; sprinkle with Parmesan and parsley. Serve hot right from skillet. Serves 6. **—Sandra Mohr, Tucson, Arizona**

ZIPPY SKILLET MACARONI

6 ounces elbow macaroni,
cooked, drained
1-1/2 cups American cheese,
shredded
1/4 cup chili sauce
1/2 teaspoon salt
1/8 teaspoon pepper
1/2 teaspoon prepared mustard
Few drops Worcestershire sauce
1/4 cup plus 1 tablespoon butter

Combine cooked macaroni, cheese and remaining ingredients EXCEPT butter. In heavy skillet melt butter; stir in macaroni mixture. Cook thoroughly over moderate heat, stirring constantly. Serves 6. **—Paula Wiebel
Atlantic, Iowa**

FAVORITE CASSEROLE

1 pound ground beef
1/2 cup onion, chopped
3/4 cup milk
1 10-3/4-ounce can cream of
mushroom soup
8 ounces cream cheese
1 17-ounce can whole kernel
corn, drained
1 4-ounce can sliced
mushrooms, drained
1/4 cup pimento, chopped
8 ounces flat noodles, cooked,
drained
1-1/2 teaspoons salt
Dash pepper

Brown meat. Add onion; cook until tender. Drain. Stir in milk, soup and cheese, blending until smooth. Add remaining ingredients. Heat to serving temperature. Serves 6. **—Lois McTaggart, Lind, Washington**

FRIED NOODLES ORIENTAL

8 ounces egg noodles, cooked, drained
1 cup oil
1 cup lean pork, cut into thin strips
1 cup carrots, thinly chopped
1 cup green beans, cut French-style
1 cup celery, thinly chopped
1/4 cup onion, chopped
1 cup bamboo shoots, optional
1 cup bean sprouts
1 tablespoon sugar
1 tablespoon salt
1/2 cup soy sauce
3 cups plus 2 tablespoons water, divided
1/4 cup green onion, chopped
1/4 cup cornstarch
2 eggs, scrambled

In large skillet or wok, fry cooked noodles in oil until delicately browned. Remove from pan; keep warm in deep serving dish. In same skillet or wok with oil from noodles, adding more oil if necessary, stir-fry pork, carrots, beans, celery, onion, bamboo shoots and bean sprouts about 5 minutes. Combine sugar, salt, soy sauce and 3 cups water; add to pork mixture. Simmer uncovered 5 minutes, then covered 2 minutes. Add green onion. Combine cornstarch and about 2 tablespoons water to make a paste; stir into vegetables. Simmer 2 minutes to thicken. Pour vegetables over noodles. **Note:** Vegetables should be tender-crisp when served. Garnish with scrambled eggs scattered over top or around edge of dish.

—Val Serrao, Davis, Illinois

GOURMET GOULASH

1 pound lean ground beef
1 cup onion, chopped
1 clove garlic, crushed
2 teaspoons salt, divided
3 cups egg noodles OR elbow macaroni, uncooked
1 20-ounce can tomato juice
1-1/2 teaspoons Worcestershire sauce
1-1/2 teaspoons celery salt
1/8 teaspoon black pepper
1 10-3/4-ounce can beef broth
1/2 cup water
1/3 cup green pepper, chopped
1 cup commercial sour cream
1 4-ounce can sliced mushrooms, drained

Saute beef, onion, garlic and 1 teaspoon salt in large skillet over medium heat. When meat is browned, add dry noodles, tomato juice, Worcestershire sauce, celery salt, black pepper, remaining 1 teaspoon salt, broth and water, mixing well. Simmer covered for 20 minutes over low heat, stirring occasionally. Add green pepper; simmer 10 minutes more or until noodles are tender. Allow to cool 3 to 4 minutes; stir in sour cream and mushrooms. Reheat slowly to serving temperature. Serves 4. **—Kathy Hommel Webster, South Dakota**

Baked 'n' Brimming

Main-Dish Pies

CHEDDAR-CRUSTED MACARONI PIE

Pastry:
- 1 cup flour
- 1/2 teaspoon salt
- 1/3 cup shortening
- 1/2 cup cheddar cheese, shredded
- 4 to 5 tablespoons ice water

Filling:
- 1/4 cup butter
- 1/4 cup flour
- 2 cups milk
- 2 tablespoons parsley, chopped
- 1 teaspoon salt
- 1/8 teaspoon cayenne pepper
- 3 ounces cream cheese, sliced
- 2 cups cheddar cheese, shredded, divided
- 1-1/2 cups elbow macaroni, cooked, drained

Pastry: Combine flour and salt. Cut in shortening until crumbly. Stir in cheese. Gradually add water; stir until flour is moistened and pastry cleans sides of bowl. Shape into a ball. On a lightly floured surface roll pastry into 11-in. circle. Line a 9-in. pie plate with pastry; flute the edge. Pierce bottom and sides of pastry with a fork. Bake 15 minutes at 425°; set aside. **Filling:** Melt butter in saucepan over low heat. Add flour; stir until smooth and bubbly. Gradually add milk, stirring constantly; cook until sauce is thick. Add parsley, salt and pepper; remove from heat. Add cream cheese and 1-1/4 cups cheddar cheese; stir until cheeses have melted. Blend in cooked macaroni. Pour mixture into pie shell. Bake at 350° for 20 minutes. Sprinkle with remaining cheddar; bake 10 to 15 minutes more. Serves 8.

—**Cynthia Kannenberg, Brown Deer, Wisconsin**

CHICKEN SYBELLA

- 2 cups chicken, cooked, diced
- 1 10-3/4-ounce can cream of chicken soup
- 1 10-3/4-ounce can chicken broth OR soup can water
- 1 4-ounce can mushrooms, drained
- 1 cup sour cream
- 1 8-ounce can sliced water chestnuts, drained
- 2-1/2 to 3 ounces spaghetti, cooked, drained
- 1/2 cup cheddar cheese, grated
- 3 tablespoons Parmesan cheese, grated
- Buttered bread crumbs
- Toasted almonds for garnish

Combine first six ingredients. Place spaghetti into baking dish. (Spaghetti layer should be about 1-1/2 in. thick.) Pour chicken mixture on top. Use a fork to gently push spaghetti just so sauce seeps in. Top with cheeses and bread crumbs. Bake at 350° until bubbly and crumbs are brown, about 30 minutes. Garnish with toasted almonds. —**Bonnie Chandler, Montross, Virginia**

SEAFOOD SPAGHETTI PIE

Crust

1 egg, beaten
1/3 cup Parmesan cheese, grated
1/4 teaspoon garlic powder

6 ounces spaghetti, cooked, drained

Filling:

3 eggs, beaten
1 4-1/2-ounce can tiny shrimp, drained
1 4-1/2-ounce can crab meat, drained, cartilage removed, flaked

1 cup evaporated skimmed milk
1/3 cup Parmesan chese, grated
2 tablespoons green onion, chopped
1/2 teaspoon dried dillweed
Paprika to taste

Crust: Combine egg, cheese and garlic powder. Add cooked spaghetti, tossing to coat well. Press mixture to form a crust in greased, 9-in pie plate; set aside. **Filling:** Combine eggs, shrimp, crab meat, milk, 1/3 cup Parmesan cheese, onion and dillweed. Pour mixture into spaghetti shell. Sprinkle with paprika. Cover edges of pie with foil. Bake at 350° for 35 to 40 minutes or until knife inserted off-center comes out clean. (Center may seem moist.) Let stand 5 minutes before serving. Serves 6.

—**Victoria L. Rinelli, Wauwatosa, Wisconsin**

SPAGHETTI PIE

6 ounces spaghetti, cooked, drained
2 tablespoons butter
2 eggs, beaten
1 cup Parmesan cheese, grated
1 tablespoon shortening
1 pound ground beef
1/2 cup onion, chopped
1/4 cup green pepper, chopped

1 cup ripe tomatoes, diced
1 6-ounce can tomato paste
1 teaspoon sugar
1/2 teaspoon dried oregano
1/2 teaspoon garlic salt
1 cup cream-style cottage cheese
8 ounces mozzarella cheese, shredded

To cooked, drained spaghetti add butter, beaten eggs and Parmesan cheese; combine thoroughly. Cover bottoms and sides of two greased, 9-in. pie plates with spaghetti mixture. Melt shortening in skillet; add ground beef, onion and green pepper. Fry until beef is browned and vegetables are tender; drain off fat. Stir in tomatoes, tomato paste, sugar, oregano and garlic salt; cook just until heated through. Spread cottage cheese over spaghetti crusts. Top with beef-tomato mixture to fill the crusts. Bake uncovered at 350° for 20 to 25 minutes. Sprinkle with mozzarella cheese; bake 5 minutes more. Serves 6. —**Debbie Sorensen, Butte, Montana**

FISH 'N' MACARONI PIE

Sauce:

2 tablespoons butter, melted
2 tablespoons flour

1/2 teaspoon salt
2-1/2 cups milk

Pie:

1-1/2 cups macaroni, cooked,
drained
1/2 cup onion, chopped

2 tablespoons parsley flakes
1 cup cheddar cheese, grated
1 pound salmon, cooked

Sauce: To melted butter in saucepan add flour and salt; gradually pour in milk. Cook, stirring constantly, until thickened. **Pie:** Place half of macaroni into greased, 1-1/2-quart casserole. Spoon 1/4 of white sauce over macaroni; sprinkle with 1/4 each of onion, parsley and cheese. Top with half of salmon; add more sauce. Sprinkle with onion, parsley and cheese. Repeat layers once, ending with cheese. Bake at 350° for 30 minutes.

—Agnes de Leon, Melrose, Montana

SPAGHETTI PAN PIE

2 tablespoons butter
2 eggs, beaten
3/4 cup Parmesan cheese, grated
8 ounces spaghetti, cooked,
drained

1-1/2 pounds ground beef
1 15-ounce jar spaghetti sauce
Salt and pepper to taste
1 cup mozzarella cheese,
shredded

Combine butter, beaten eggs and Parmesan cheese; add to cooked spaghetti. Place mixture into greased, 12- x 8-in. casserole. Brown and drain ground beef; stir in spaghetti sauce, salt and pepper. Spoon meat sauce over spaghetti. Bake at 350° for 20 minutes. Top with mozzarella cheese; bake 10 minutes more. Cut into squares, or serve casserole-style.

—Lois Watermeier, Unadilla, Nebraska

CHEESY SPAGHETTI PIE

16 ounces spaghetti, cooked,
drained
1-1/2 pounds sausage OR ground
beef, browned, drained
6 eggs, beaten

24 ounces mozzarella cheese,
grated
1 teaspoon oregano
1/4 teaspoon each salt and pepper
1 15-ounce jar spaghetti sauce
OR homemade sauce

Combine all ingredients EXCEPT spaghetti sauce. Pat firmly into heavy, 10-in. skillet; cook over low heat on stovetop until browned on bottom, about 30 minutes. Flip to other side; brown. **Note:** Recipe may also be made in oven, baking at 350° for 1 hour. Serve in wedges, topped with spaghetti sauce. Serves 8. **—Suzanne Nicklas, Stoneham, Colorado**

44

PASGHETTI PIZZA

Crust:
2 eggs
1/2 cup milk
1 cup mozzarella cheese, shredded

3/4 teaspoon garlic powder
1/2 teaspoon salt
16 ounces spaghetti, cooked, drained

Topping:
32 ounces spaghetti sauce
1-1/2 teaspoons oregano

3 cups mozzarella cheese, shredded
Pepperoni, sliced

Crust: Combine eggs, milk, mozzarella, garlic powder, salt and cooked spaghetti. Spread into greased, 15- x 10- x 1-in. jelly roll pan. Bake at 350° for 15 minutes. **Topping:** Combine spaghetti sauce and oregano. Spread sauce evenly over partially baked spaghetti mixture; sprinkle with 3 cups cheese. Arrange pepperoni slices over top. Bake 30 minutes more. Let cool 5 minutes before cutting. **—Carol Imhoff, Rittman, Ohio**

Jiffy Jumbo Shells

STUFFED SHELLS SUPREME

20 jumbo shells
1 tablespoon oil

Sauce:
1 pound loose sausage
2 tablespoons olive oil
1/2 cup onion, chopped
1 teaspoon garlic, minced
3 cups tomatoes, chopped

1 6-ounce can tomato paste
1 teaspoon oregano
1 teaspoon sugar
1 teaspoon salt

Filling:
3 cups ricotta cheese
2 cups mozzarella cheese, shredded
1/2 cup Parmesan cheese, grated

2 eggs
1 teaspoon salt
1 teaspoon oregano

Sauce: Brown sausage in olive oil. Add onion; cook until onion is fairly soft. Add remaining ingredients; simmer uncovered 30 minutes, stirring occasionally. Meanwhile, boil jumbo shells in 3 quarts water with 1 tablespoon oil added. Cook 20 minutes; drain. **Filling:** Combine cheeses, eggs, salt and oregano. Cover bottom of baking dish with thin layer of sauce. Fill each shell with cheese filling. Arrange shells over sauce, open side up. Pour remaining sauce over shells. Bake at 350° for 45 minutes.

—Debbie Taylor, Allenwood, Pennsylvania

SHELLS FLORENTINE

10 ounces jumbo shells, cooked, drained
1/2 cup onion, minced
1 clove garlic, crushed
2 tablespoons butter
2 cups cottage cheese
1 10-ounce package frozen, chopped spinach, thawed, well drained
2 eggs, slightly beaten
1/2 teaspoon salt
1 teaspoon basil leaves, crushed
1-1/2 cups cheddar cheese, shredded
1 15-ounce jar meatless spaghetti sauce
1/2 cup water
1/4 cup Parmesan cheese, grated

Cover cooked, drained shells with cold water until ready to stuff. Saute onion and garlic in butter until onion is tender. Beat cottage cheese with mixer on high about 5 minutes. Add onion and garlic, spinach, eggs, salt, basil and cheddar cheese; combine thoroughly. Drain shells; stuff with cottage cheese filling. Combine spaghetti sauce and water; pour enough sauce into a 13- x 9- x 2-in. baking dish to just cover the bottom. Place stuffed shells stuffing side up on top of sauce; pour on remaining sauce. Sprinkle with Parmesan cheese; bake at 350° for 40 to 45 minutes or until hot and bubbly. Serves 6.   **—Leila Briggs, Arkport, New York**

STUFFED SHELLS

12 ounces jumbo shells, cooked, drained
1/2 pound Italian sweet sausage OR mild pork sausage
1 quart spaghetti sauce
2 eggs, beaten
2 10-ounce packages frozen, chopped spinach, thawed, well drained
16 ounces ricotta cheese OR cottage cheese
8 ounces mozzarella cheese, shredded
1 teaspoon onion salt
1/4 teaspoon garlic powder OR salt
1/8 teaspoon nutmeg
2 tablespoons Parmesan cheese, grated

Cover cooked, drained shells with cold water. Set aside. Brown crumbled sausage in skillet; drain off fat. Add spaghetti sauce. Cover; simmer 15 minutes. In large bowl thoroughly combine beaten eggs, spinach, ricotta, mozzarella, onion salt, garlic and nutmeg. Pour about 1/2 cup sauce mixture into 3-quart or larger casserole. Stuff each shell with 2 heaping teaspoons of spinach-cheese mixture. Arrange shells in single layer, stuffed side up. Pour remaining sauce over shells; sprinkle with Parmesan cheese. Bake covered at 350° for 20 minutes, then uncovered for 10 minutes or until bubbly. **Note:** This becomes a vegetarian dish if the sausage is omitted.

—Corinne Rickabaugh, Shreve, Ohio

JUMBO DELIGHT

Manicotti noodles (about 27),
    cooked, drained

Filling:

32 ounces ricotta	2 eggs
8 ounces mozzarella cheese, cubed	1 tablespoon parsley, snipped
	1 teaspoon salt
1/3 cup Parmesan cheese, grated	1/4 teaspoon pepper

Sauce:

1 cup onion, minced	1 35-ounce can Italian
1 clove garlic, crushed	tomatoes, undrained
1/4 cup olive oil	1 6-ounce can tomato paste
1 teaspoon oregano	2 tablespoons parsley, snipped
1/2 teaspoon basil	1 tablespoon salt
1/4 teaspoon pepper	2 teaspoons sugar
1-1/2 cups water	

Sauce: Saute onion and garlic in oil. Add remaining ingredients; simmer 1 hour. **Filling:** Combine all ingredients. Stuff shells. Pour 1 cup of sauce into 13- x 9-in. baking pan. Place noodles on top of sauce. Pour remaining sauce over shells. Bake at 350º for 30 minutes or until bubbly.

—**Barbara A. Hill, Rockford, Illinois**

TUFULIS

1 clove garlic, crushed	1 egg
1/2 teaspoon salt	1 cup bread crumbs
1 medium onion, minced	Dash pepper
1 2-ounce can mushroom pieces, drained	1/4 teaspoon oregano
	Manicotti noodles (about 24),
2 tablespoons cooking oil	cooked, drained
3/4 pound Italian sausage	3 8-ounce cans tomato sauce
3/4 pound ground beef	Parmesan cheese, grated
8 ounces mozzarella cheese, cubed	

Combine garlic and salt. Saute onion and mushrooms in cooking oil with garlic and salt, cooking until onion is tender. In large mixing bowl combine meats, cheese, egg, bread crumbs, pepper, oregano and vegetables from skillet. Stuff noodles. Place into two 13- x 9-in. baking pans, making a single layer in each pan. Pour tomato sauce over the noodles. Sprinkle with Parmesan. Bake covered at 350º for 30 to 35 minutes. **Note:** Tufulis are just as good reheated. —**Debbie Swier, Edgerton, Minnesota**

HAM-STUFFED MANICOTTI

1/4 cup onion, chopped
2 tablespoons oil
3 cups ham, cooked, ground
3 2-ounce cans chopped
  mushrooms, drained
3 tablespoons Parmesan cheese,
  grated

1/4 cup green pepper, chopped
3 tablespoons butter
3 tablespoons flour
2 cups milk
1 cup Swiss cheese, shredded
8 manicotti shells, cooked, drained
Paprika

Saute onion in oil until tender. Add ham and mushrooms. Remove from heat; cool a few minutes. Stir in Parmesan cheese; set aside. Saute green pepper in butter until tender. Blend in flour. Add milk; cook until thick and bubbly. Stir in Swiss cheese until melted. Combine 1/4 cup cheese sauce with ham and mushroom mixture. Fill shells; place in 11- x 7-in. baking dish. Pour remaining cheese sauce over top of shells. Sprinkle with paprika. Bake covered at 350° for 35 minutes. Serves 4.

—Jeane Downing, Cambridge, Illinois

CHICKEN-FILLED SHELLS

2 cups chicken, cooked, diced
1 cup peas, cooked, drained
1/2 cup mayonnaise
1/3 cup onion, finely chopped
Salt and pepper to taste

12 ounces jumbo shell macaroni,
  cooked, drained
1/2 cup water
1 10-3/4-ounce can cream of
  mushroom soup

Combine chicken, peas, mayonnaise and onion; salt and pepper to taste. Stuff shells with chicken mixture; arrange shells in single layer in baking dish. Add water to soup; pour over shells. Cover baking dish with foil. Bake at 325° for 30 minutes. Serves 8. **—Karen Schmidt, Racine, Wisconsin**

MEXICAN GREEN PEPPERS

6 medium green peppers
1 pound ground beef
1 large onion, chopped
1-1/3 cups fresh tomato, chopped

1 cup macaroni, cooked, drained
1-1/2 teaspoons salt
1 teaspoon chili powder
1 8-ounce can tomato sauce

Cut off tops of green peppers; remove seeds. Cook peppers for 5 minutes in boiling, salted water to cover. Drain; set aside. Combine next 6 ingredients; mix well. Fill peppers with meat mixture; place in shallow, 2-quart casserole. Pour tomato sauce over and around peppers. Bake at 375° for 45 to 50 minutes. Serves 6. **—Mabel O. Ripperdan, Urbana, Illinois**

Layers
Unlimited

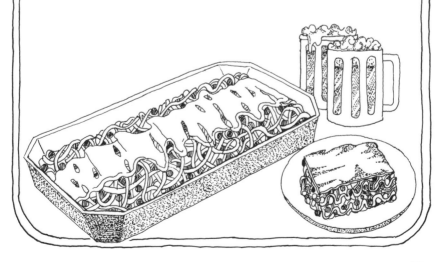

Spaghetti Toppers

TUNA TETRAZZINI

3 tablespoons onion, chopped
2 tablespoons butter
1 10-3/4 ounce can cream of
mushroom soup
3 tablespoons dry white wine
1/2 cup water
1/2 cup romano cheese, divided

1 6-1/2 ounce can tuna fish,
drained
1 tablespoon parsley, snipped
2 teaspoons lemon juice
8 ounces spaghetti, cooked,
drained

Saute onion in butter until golden brown. Add soup, wine, water and 1/4 cup romano cheese. Stir in tuna, parsley and lemon juice; heat thoroughly. Combine tuna mixture and spaghetti. Place into greased, 2-quart casserole; top with 1/4 cup romano cheese. Heat under broiler until golden brown. **Note:** Chicken pieces may be substituted for tuna. Fresh mushrooms may be added. **—Patsy Moody, Hamden, New York**

SHAFFER BAKED SPAGHETTI

8 slices bacon
1 onion, chopped
1/3 green pepper, chopped
2 pounds ground beef
1 16-ounce can whole tomatoes
1 12-ounce can tomato paste
1 6-ounce can pitted, ripe olives,
chopped, drained
1 4-ounce can sliced mushrooms,
drained

1 teaspoon Worcestershire
sauce
1 tablespoon chili powder
2 tablespoons sugar
Salt and pepper to taste
Dash garlic powder
16 ounces vermicelli, cooked,
drained
Parmesan cheese, grated

Fry bacon in skillet. Remove bacon; saute onion and green pepper until tender in drippings. Add ground beef; cook for 10 minutes or until brown. Drain. Add tomatoes, tomato paste, olives, mushrooms, Worcestershire sauce and seasonings. Cook uncovered over low heat for 1 hour. In a 13- x 9-in., greased baking dish layer cooked pasta, meat sauce and Parmesan, repeating layers until all ingredients are used. Top with crumbled bacon. Bake at 450° for 20 to 30 minutes, until golden brown.
—Joyce A. O'Dell, Orrick, Missouri

LONG PASTA: *When cooking long pastas such as spaghetti, immerse them gradually in boiling water. The portion of each noodle covered by water will soften, making room to push the pasta further and further into the water.*

SPAGHETTI AND SALMON DELUXE

2 cups tomato, chopped
1 teaspoon onion, minced
1 teaspoon salt
1/4 teaspoon pepper
1 teaspoon sugar
1 tablespoon flour

2 tablespoons butter
4 ounces spaghetti,
  cooked, drained
1 cup salmon
1/2 cup buttered bread crumbs

Combine tomato, onion, salt and pepper, sugar, flour and butter in saucepan; simmer 10 minutes. Layer half each of spaghetti, then salmon, then tomato mixture in baking dish; repeat layers. Sprinkle with buttered bread crumbs. Bake at 400° for 30 minutes.

—Agnes de Leon, Melrose, Montana

BROCCOLI TETRAZZINI

1-1/3 cups spaghetti, cooked,
  drained
2 cups chopped broccoli,
  cooked, drained
1 8-ounce can chopped
  mushrooms, drained

1 cup evaporated milk
1/2 cup water
4 ounces American cheese,
  shredded
Dash hot sauce
Dash Worcestershire sauce

In 2-quart, round casserole layer spaghetti, then broccoli, then mushrooms. In medium-sized saucepan combine evaporated milk and water; heat, gradually stirring in cheese. When sauce is well blended, stir in hot sauce and Worcestershire sauce. Pour over mushroom layer in casserole. Bake at 350° for 40 to 45 minutes. Serves 4.   —Anna Rothchild, Beloit, Kansas

SPAGHETTI PIZZA BAKE

16 ounces spaghetti
2 eggs, lightly beaten
3/4 cup milk
4 cups mozzarella cheese,
  shredded, divided

1/2 teaspoon salt
1 quart spaghetti sauce
1-1/2 teaspoons oregano
3-1/2 ounces sliced pepperoni

Break spaghetti into pieces 2 to 3 inches long; cook according to package directions. Drain; cool. In large bowl combine lightly beaten eggs, milk, 1 cup mozzarella and salt. Add spaghetti; stir until noodles are evenly coated. Fold mixture into greased, 14- x 12-in. broiler pan or 15- x 10-in. jelly roll pan. Spread spaghetti sauce over noodle mixture. Sprinkle with oregano, then 3 cups mozzarella. Top with pepperoni slices. Bake at 350° for 30 to 45 minutes. Let stand at room temperature for 5 minutes before cutting.

—Ruthie Horob, Williston, North Dakota

Noodles Upon Noodles

MACARONI PIZZA

1 pound ground beef
1 medium onion, finely chopped
1 15-ounce can tomato sauce
1 teaspoon salt, divided
1/2 teaspoon oregano
1/4 teaspoon pepper
1/2 teaspoon garlic powder
1/2 cup milk
1 egg
2 cups macaroni, cooked, drained
1/4 to 1/2 pound mozzarella OR
cheddar cheese, shredded

Saute ground beef and onion; drain off fat. Add tomato sauce, 1/2 teaspoon salt and remaining seasonings; simmer 5 to 10 minutes. Beat together milk, egg and 1/2 teaspoon salt. Blend into macaroni; place noodle mixture into greased, 15- x 10-in. pan. Cover with meat mixture. Top with cheese. Bake at 350° for 20 minutes; let stand 5 to 10 minutes before cutting. Serves 6. **Note:** Leftover roast or sausage may be substituted for ground beef.

—Lyla Getting, Fulda, Minnesota

CHICKEN-SAUSAGE SUPREME

6 ounces wide noodles, cooked,
drained
1/2 pound sausage
1 small onion, chopped
1 3-pound chicken, cooked,
boned, chopped
1 10-3/4-ounce can vegetable
soup
1 8-3/4-ounce can whole kernel
corn
8 ounces cheese, grated, divided

Place cooked noodles into 13- x 9- x 2-in. casserole. Brown sausage and onion; drain. Add chicken; blend in soup and corn. Stir in half of cheese. Pour sausage mixture over noodles; top with remaining cheese. Bake at 350° for 15 to 20 minutes or until cheese melts.   **—Linda Babcock, Groom, Texas**

BEANS 'N' MACARONI

1/2 pound ground beef
1 medium onion, finely chopped
1 16-ounce can pork 'n' beans OR
great northerns
1 10-3/4-ounce can tomato soup
1/4 cup barbecue sauce
1/3 cup ketchup
8 ounces shell macaroni, cooked,
drained
5 slices cheese

In skillet brown beef and onion; drain. Mix beans, tomato soup, barbecue sauce and ketchup. Cover bottom of greased, 2-quart casserole with sauce. Layer macaroni, then beef and onion, then more sauce. Top with cheese slices; bake at 375° for 30 minutes or until bubbly hot.

—Donna M. Davis, Harmony, North Carolina

REUBEN BAKE

8 ounces egg noodles, cooked, drained
4 tablespoons butter, divided
1 16-ounce can sauerkraut
1 12-ounce can corned beef, shredded
1/2 cup salad dressing
1 large tomato, sliced
2 cups Swiss cheese, shredded
1/2 cup cracker crumbs
1/4 teaspoon caraway seeds

Place hot noodles into 13- x 9-in. baking dish. Add 2 tablespoons butter; toss to coat noodles. Spread sauerkraut over noodles. Top with corned beef, followed by dressing, tomato and cheese. Melt 2 tablespoons butter; toss in cracker crumbs and caraway seeds. Sprinkle crumb mixture over cheese layer. Bake at 350° for about 1 hour, until hot and bubbly. Serves 6.
—**Jacqueline Keenan, Hudson, Michigan**

PIZZA BAKE

1 pound lean ground beef
1 large onion, chopped
1/2 teaspoon salt
Dash pepper
8 ounces elbow macaroni, cooked, drained
1 15-ounce jar spaghetti sauce
1/4 pound pepperoni, thinly sliced
8 ounces mozzarella cheese, grated
1 4-ounce can mushrooms, drained, optional

Brown meat with onion; season with salt and pepper. Combine drained meat mixture, macaroni and spaghetti sauce. Place half of mixture into greased, 13- x 9-in. baking dish. Top with half each of pepperoni and cheese. All the mushrooms may be added to the casserole at this point, if desired. Repeat layers, except for mushrooms. Bake uncovered at 350° for 30 minutes.   —**Stella M. Rewa, South Deerfield, Massachusetts**

MACARONI DELUXE

7 ounces macaroni, cooked, drained
1 tablespoon onion, minced
1 tablespoon green pepper, chopped
Salt to taste
12 soda crackers, crushed
1 cup canned tomatoes
6 slices process cheese
1/2 cup cream

To cooked, drained pasta add onion, peppers and salt. Place half of noodles into a 2-quart casserole. Sprinkle with half of cracker crumbs, then 1/2 cup tomatoes. Top with 3 slices cheese. Repeat layers once. Pour cream over all. Bake covered at 350° for 25 to 30 minutes. Bake uncovered until golden brown on top, 5 to 10 minutes more. Serves 6.
—**Mrs. Eddie Paulson, Powers Lake, North Dakota**

HUNTINGTON CHICKEN

4 cups chicken, cooked, cubed
5 cups chicken broth
2 cubes chicken bouillon
1 cup onion, chopped
2/3 cup celery, chopped
2 teaspoons salt
1/2 teaspoon pepper
1/2 teaspoon poultry seasoning

3/4 cup cream
1/4 cup flour
4 cups elbow OR shell macaroni, cooked, drained
8 ounces Velveeta cheese, sliced
1/2 cup butter
2 cups bread crumbs

In 4-quart saucepan combine chicken, broth, bouillon cubes, onion, celery, salt, pepper and poultry seasoning. Cook until vegetables are tender. Combine cream and flour; stir into chicken mixture. Bring to boil. Remove from heat; set aside. Into greased, 6-quart baking dish place half each of macaroni, then chicken mixture, then cheese. Repeat layers once. Bake at 325º about 35 minutes. Meanwhile, melt 1/2 cup butter in skillet. Add bread crumbs; cook, stirring, until lightly browned. Top mixture in baking dish with crumbs; bake 10 minutes more. Serves 12.

—Elsie Troyer, Paris, Tennessee

CHICKEN TETRAZZINI

Sauce:
1/2 cup butter, melted
1/3 cup flour
1-1/2 teaspoons salt
1/8 teaspoon garlic powder

1 cup chicken broth
2 cups half-and-half cream
2 tablespoons sherry

Casserole:
8 ounces egg noodles, cooked, drained
1/2 cup plus 2 tablespoons Parmesan cheese, grated

1 4-ounce can sliced mushrooms, drained
2 cups chicken, cooked, cubed

Sauce: To melted butter add flour, salt and garlic. Add chicken broth and cream. Cook over low heat, stirring constantly, until thick and smooth; stir in sherry. **Casserole:** Place 1/3 of noodles into a casserole dish; sprinkle with 2 tablespoons Parmesan. Top with 1/3 each of mushrooms and chicken. Pour 1 cup sherry sauce over top. Repeat layers twice more. Top with remaining 1/4 cup Parmesan cheese; bake at 350º for 30 minutes.

—Peggy Calhoon, Greensburg, Kentucky

ENOUGH WATER: *A 7-quart kettle will accommodate 1 pound of pasta without crowding. Add 1 tablespoon salt for seasoning and 1 tablespoon olive oil to keep pasta from sticking together.*

SPANISH EGGS

1/2 cup onion, chopped
1/2 cup green pepper, chopped
3 tablespoons plus 1/4 cup
butter, divided
2-1/2 cups canned tomatoes with
juice
4 ounces American cheese,
grated
1/4 cup flour
1/2 teaspoon salt
Pepper to taste
6 ounces egg noodles, cooked,
drained
6 hard-cooked eggs, sliced

Saute onions and green pepper in 3 tablespoons butter until tender; do not brown. Add tomatoes; simmer 10 to 15 minutes. Blend in cheese. Melt 1/4 cup butter; stir in flour, salt and pepper. Add to tomato mixture; cook, stirring, until thickened. Spread half of noodles over bottom of greased, 11- x 7-x 2-in. baking dish. Arrange egg slices from 3 eggs over noodles. Top with half of tomato mixture. Repeat layers once. Bake at 350º for 25 minutes. Serves 6.   **—Dora E. Rupnow, Jefferson, Wisconsin**

Novelty Bakes

MOM'S GILBERTINI

Casserole:

1 pound sausage, browned,
drained
1 cup each of 3 novelty pastas
cooked, drained
1 4-ounce can mushrooms,
drained

Sauce:

1/2 cup green onion, diced
1/4 cup butter
1/4 cup flour
1/2 teaspoon salt
Dash pepper
1 teaspoon Italian seasoning
3 cups milk
2 cups mozzarella cheese,
shredded, divided
1/2 cup Parmesan cheese, grated

Casserole: Combine sausage, pasta and mushrooms; place into greased casserole. **Sauce:** Saute onion in butter until tender but not brown. Stir in flour, salt, pepper and Italian seasoning. Gradually add milk; cook, stirring, until thick and bubbly. Stir in 1-1/2 cups mozzarella cheese; remove from heat when cheese is just melted. Pour over pasta mixture; top with remaining cheeses. Cover with foil; bake at 375º for 25 minutes. Remove the foil; bake 10 minutes more or until heated through.

—Priscilla J. Root, Belle Plaine, Iowa

GREEN-NOODLE BAKE

1 10-ounce package frozen
  asparagus, cooked, drained
16 ounces green noodles, cooked,
  drained
Parmesan cheese, grated
Chicken or turkey pieces, cooked
1 cup mushrooms, sliced
Salt and pepper to taste
2 10-3/4-ounce cans cream of
  chicken soup
1 cup milk
3 tablespoons butter

Place all the cooked asparagus into large casserole. Cover with some of noodles; sprinkle with cheese. Top with chicken or turkey pieces; add layer of mushroom slices. Season lightly with salt and pepper. Combine soup and milk; pour part of soup mixture over top. Repeat layers until casserole is filled to within 1 in. of top. Sprinkle top liberally with cheese; dot with butter. Bake at 350° for 45 minutes or until golden brown and bubbly. Serves 4.

—Gladys Nourse, Sheffield, Massachusetts

PATES BONNE FEMME

1 onion, chopped
1-1/2 tablespoons butter
9 ounces novelty noodles,
  cooked, drained, reserving
  1 cup water
1 cube bouillon
Salt and pepper to taste
1 cup ground beef, browned,
  drained OR bacon, cooked,
  drained, crumbled
1/2 cup Swiss cheese, grated

Saute onion in 1-1/2 tablespoons butter. Add water reserved from cooking pasta; toss in bouillon cube. Simmer uncovered 10 minutes, stirring constantly. Add drained pasta; sprinkle with salt and pepper to taste. Simmer 5 minutes. In greased baking pan layer pasta mixture, meat and cheese. Dot with butter. Broil 5 minutes or until cheese makes a golden crust.

—Dianne Dunham, Whitewater, Wisconsin

HAMBURGER-NOODLE CASSEROLE

1 pound ground beef
1/2 cup onion, chopped
1/2 cup celery, chopped
1 10-3/4-ounce can cream of
  chicken soup
1 10-3/4-ounce can tomato soup
1 soup can milk
1/2 cup frozen peas
1/2 cup frozen corn
Salt and pepper to taste
2 cups noodles, cooked, drained

Brown ground beef with onion and celery. In saucepan heat remaining ingredients EXCEPT noodles; stir in meat, onion and celery. In 1-1/2-quart casserole place half of meat-vegetable mixture. Spoon in cooked noodles; top with remaining meat-vegetable mixture. Bake at 350° for 30 minutes.

—Paula L. Stene, Joliet, Montana

CREAMY NOODLE BAKE

1/2 cup butter
5 tablespoons flour
1 teaspoon salt
1/4 teaspoon pepper
2-1/2 cups milk
8 ounces cream cheese, sliced

1/2 cup olives stuffed with
    pimentos, sliced
2 tablespoons chives
8 ounces noodles, cooked,
    drained
6 ounces muenster cheese,
    sliced

In 1-1/2-quart saucepan melt butter. Stir in flour, salt and pepper; cook until bubbly, stirring constantly. Add milk; stir until thickened. Boil 1 minute. Add cream cheese slices to sauce; stir until cheese is melted. Add olives and chives; remove from heat. Spread half of cheese mixture over bottom of greased, 13- x 9-in. baking dish. Top with half the noodles. Place half the muenster cheese slices over noodles. Repeat layers once. Bake at 350° for 30 to 35 minutes or until golden brown and bubbly.

—Elaine Brown, Prumzurlay, West Germany (APO, New York)

CAVATINI

1 15-ounce can tomato sauce
1/4 teaspoon garlic salt
1/2 teaspoon oregano
1/2 teaspoon salt
1 teaspoon basil leaves
1/4 cup Parmesan cheese
2-1/2 cups novelty pasta, cooked,
    drained

1 pound pork sausage,
    browned, drained
1 4-ounce can sliced
    mushrooms, drained
1/2 cup pepperoni, sliced
1/2 cup onion, chopped
1/2 cup green pepper,
    finely chopped
1 cup mozzarella cheese, grated

Combine tomato sauce, garlic salt, oregano, salt, basil leaves and Parmesan cheese in blender; mix well. Place cooked macaroni into 2-quart baking dish. Pour on half the tomato sauce mixture; top with pork sausage, mushrooms and pepperoni. Pour remaining sauce over all; sprinkle with onion and green pepper, then mozzarella cheese. Bake at 350° for 30 minutes.

—Dianne Hendricks, Vivian, South Dakota

PASTA WITH BROCCOLI

2 cups half-and-half
    cream
2 cloves garlic, minced
16 ounces rigatoni OR mostaccioli
    noodles, cooked, drained
1/2 cup tomato sauce, optional
1/2 cup butter

16 ounces fresh broccoli OR 1
    18-ounce package frozen
    broccoli, cooked, drained
1/2 to 1 cup Parmesan cheese,
    grated
Pepper to taste

◄| CONTINUED ON NEXT PAGE |►

Add cream and garlic to cooked, drained noodles. Stir in tomato sauce, if desired; bring to boil. Add butter; after butter melts, add cooked broccoli. Remove from heat. Just before serving, toss with Parmesan; sprinkle with pepper to taste. **Note:** When reheating add cream or tomato sauce.

—Sophie N. Smith, St. Ann, Missouri

NOODLE SURPRISE

1/2 pound veal, cut into bite-size
   pieces
1/2 pound pork, cut into bite-size
   pieces
1/2 cup water
   2 or 3 stalks celery, chopped
   1 small onion, chopped
Salt and pepper to taste
   8 ounces noodles, cooked,
   drained

1 8-3/4-ounce can cream-style
   corn
1 10-3/4-ounce can cream of
   mushroom soup
1 2-ounce can mushrooms,
   drained
Buttered cracker crumbs for
   topping, optional

Saute veal and pork in a skillet to brown slightly. Add 1/2 cup water, celery, onion and salt and pepper to taste. Cook covered, stewing for 2 hours or until meat is done. Place cooked, drained noodles into 12- x 8- x 2-in. baking dish. Top with meat mixture, corn, soup and mushrooms. Bake at 300° for 1 hour. Just before serving, top with buttered cracker crumbs. Serves 4.

—Mrs. Dale Markwardt, Manitowoc, Wisconsin

Luscious Lasagnas

LASAGNA

1 pound ground beef
3/4 tablespoon onion, chopped
2 tablespoons oil
1 16-ounce can tomatoes
2 6-ounce cans tomato paste
2 cups water
1 tablespoon parsley, ground
2 teaspoons salt
1 teaspoon sugar

1 teaspoon garlic powder
1/2 teaspoon pepper
1/2 teaspoon oregano
16 ounces lasagna noodles,
   cooked, drained
16 ounces ricotta cheese
8 ounces mozzarella cheese,
   shredded
1 cup Parmesan cheese, grated

Brown beef and onion in oil. Add tomatoes, tomato paste, water, parsley, salt, sugar, garlic powder, pepper and oregano. Simmer 45 minutes. In greased, 13- x 9- x 2-in. baking dish layer half each of noodles, sauce, then ricotta and mozzarella cheeses. Repeat layers. Sprinkle Parmesan over top. Bake at 350° for 30 to 45 minutes. **—Ramona Rizzo, Cleveland, Mississippi**

TOFU LASAGNA

8 ounces fresh mushrooms,
thinly sliced
1/4 cup butter
3 cloves garlic, finely crushed
1/2 teaspoon salt
1/8 teaspoon pepper
3 cups purchased spaghetti sauce
1/2 cup wheat germ

1 cup tofu, mashed
1/4 cup Parmesan cheese, grated
8 ounces mozzarella cheese,
shredded
1/4 cup parsley, snipped
8 ounces lasagna noodles,
cooked, drained

Saute mushrooms in 1/4 cup butter with garlic, salt and pepper. Cook until mushrooms are tender. Stir in spaghetti sauce and wheat germ; heat thoroughly. Combine tofu and Parmesan in one bowl; combine mozzarella and parsley in another bowl. Place 1/3 of cooked lasagna noodles into 12- x 8-in. baking dish. Spread half of tofu mixture over top. Pour on 1/3 of spaghetti sauce. Top with 1/3 mozzarella mixture. Repeat layers. End with a third layer of lasagna noodles, sauce, then mozzarella mixture. Bake at 350° for 45 minutes or until hot and bubbly. Let stand 15 minutes before cutting. Garnish with parsley, if desired. **Note:** Allow an extra 15 minutes for baking if lasagna is made ahead and stored in the refrigerator. Serves 8.

—Karen Schmidt, Racine, Wisconsin

ZESTY LASAGNA

1/2 pound Italian sausage
1 pound ground beef
1 clove garlic, minced
1 tablespoon dried basil, crushed
1 teaspoon oregano
2 teaspoons salt, divided
3/4 teaspoon pepper, divided
1 onion, chopped
3 tablespoons mushrooms,
chopped
3 cups canned tomatoes

2 6-ounce cans tomato paste
10 ounces lasagna noodles,
cooked, drained
3 cups ricotta cheese
1/2 cup Parmesan cheese, grated
2 tablespoons dried parsley
flakes
2 eggs, beaten
8 ounces mozzarella cheese,
shredded

Brown sausage and ground beef together; drain fat. Add garlic, basil, oregano, 1 teaspoon salt, 1/4 teaspoon pepper, onion, mushrooms, tomatoes and tomato paste. Simmer uncovered 30 minutes, stirring occasionally. While noodles are cooking, combine ricotta cheese, Parmesan, parsley, eggs, 1 teaspoon salt and 1/2 teaspoon pepper. Place half of cooked noodles into 13- x 9- x 2-in. baking dish. Spread with half each of ricotta filling, then mozzarella, then tomato sauce. Repeat layers. Bake at 375° about 30 minutes. Let stand 10 minutes before cutting. Serves 8.

—Janice Rinne, Stockton, California

LOW-CAL WHITE LASAGNA FLORENTINE

2-1/2 cups skim milk
   3 tablespoons instant-blending
     flour
1-1/2 teaspoons salt
Pepper to taste
   1/4 teaspoon nutmeg
Pinch cayenne pepper OR dash
     Tabasco
     2 10-ounce packages frozen,
      chopped spinach, cooked,
      drained

8 protein-enriched lasagna
   noodles, cooked, drained
8 ounces low-fat cottage cheese
2 hard-cooked eggs, thinly
   sliced
2 tablespoons Parmesan
   cheese, grated
2 tablespoons Italian-seasoned
   bread crumbs

In saucepan combine milk and flour; cook, stirring, until thickened. Add seasonings. Blend half of white sauce into cooked spinach. Pour a thin layer of sauce over bottom of shallow baking pan. Arrange 4 cooked noodles over sauce; top with half of spinach mixture. Add half each of cottage cheese and egg slices. Repeat layers. Top with remaining white sauce; sprinkle with Parmesan and bread crumbs. Bake at 375º for 30 to 40 minutes. Serves 6 at under 200 calories per serving.

—Florence Lorence, Racine, Wisconsin

NOODLES 'N' CHEESE

   8 ounces lasagna noodles
   1 tablespoon butter
   1 teaspoon salt
Dash pepper
1/4 cup milk
   1 tablespoon parsley flakes
   1 egg, beaten

4 ounces small curd cottage
   cheese
2 ounces mozzarella cheese,
   shredded
4 ounces Swiss cheese, cut into
   squares
1/2 cup bread crumbs
   3 tablespoons butter

Parboil noodles; place half of noodles into greased loaf pan, cutting pasta to size. Combine butter, salt, pepper, milk, parsley flakes and egg; stir in cottage cheese. Top first layer of lasagna noodles with half of mozzarella, 1/3 egg-cottage cheese mixture, then half of Swiss cheese. Repeat layers once. Top with remaining egg-cottage cheese mixture. Sprinkle with bread crumbs; dot with butter. Bake at 375º for 45 minutes or until top is golden brown.

—Sandra S. Page, Rochelle, Illinois

HOMEMADE NOODLES: *After rolling out noodle dough, let dry until firm but still pliable. When making noodles ahead of time, store air-dried pasta in plastic bags until ready to use.*

SLIM 'N' TRIM TUNA LASAGNA

1/2 cup onion, chopped
2 tablespoons butter, melted
2 6-1/2-ounce cans water-
 packed tuna, well drained
1 10-3/4-ounce can cream of
 mushroom soup
1/2 cup skim milk
1-1/2 cups cottage cheese

1/2 teaspoon garlic salt
1/2 teaspoon oregano
1/4 teaspoon pepper
8 ounces lasagna noodles,
 cooked, drained
8 ounces Swiss OR mozzarella
 cheese, thinly sliced
1/4 cup Parmesan cheese, grated

Saute onion in butter; add tuna, soup, milk, cottage cheese and seasonings. Into greased, 12- x 8-in. baking dish place half each of noodles, tuna mixture and Swiss or mozzarella cheese. Repeat layers. Sprinkle Parmesan cheese over top. Bake at 350° for 30 minutes; let cool 5 minutes before cutting. Serves 6 at about 275 calories per 1-1/2-cup serving.

—Adeline Lerum, Seymour, Wisconsin

YUMMY CRAB LASAGNA

8 ounces lasagna noodles,
 cooked, drained
2 10-3/4-ounce cans shrimp soup
2 4-1/4-ounce cans crab meat
2 cups small curd cottage cheese
8 ounces cream cheese

1 egg
2 teaspoons basil
1 medium onion, chopped
Salt and pepper to taste
3 tomatoes, cut into thin slices
1/2 cup cheddar cheese, shredded

Cover cooked noodles with cold water. Heat together shrimp soup and crab meat. Blend cottage cheese, cream cheese, egg, basil, onion, salt and pepper. Spread half of cheese mixture in greased casserole. Top with half of noodles, then all of shrimp soup and crab meat mixture. Add another layer of noodles, remaining cheese mixture, then a layer of tomato slices. Bake 15 minutes at 350°. Sprinkle with cheddar cheese; return to oven for 30 minutes more or until golden brown and bubbly.

—Mrs. Clifford Haynes, Melba, Idaho

LASAGNA NOODLES

1 cup flour
1/4 teaspoon salt

2 egg whites
Water

Combine flour, salt and egg whites; mix well. Add small amounts of water until dough forms a soft ball. Divide dough in half. Roll each half to 1/4 in. thick on floured board. Cut into strips 2 in. wide and 4 to 6 in. long. Cook in 2 quarts salted water for 3 to 5 minutes. Use in any lasagna recipe.

—Karen Schmidt, Racine, Wisconsin

Index

QUICK CASSEROLES

STOVETOP SPECIALTIES

More Family-Favorite Recipes and Kitchen Helpers!

BAR COOKIE BONANZA. Cookies are a must in most country families —and this cookbook lets you make quick work of their making. Includes *150 fast and easy* country favorites...chocolate, butterscotch, caramel, oatmeal, nuts, cereal and more!
#0205 *Bar Cookie Bonanza* cookbook **$4.98**

HOMEMADE BREADS. A country meal isn't complete without bread! Book includes *100 "farm-tested"* recipes for white, wheat, rye, herb, onion, cheese, oatmeal breads and more! Plus, "helpful hints" for "starters" as well as bread-baking "pros".
#0190 *Homemade Breads* cookbook..**$4.98**

WOOD BREAD SLICER. You'll cut your next loaf of homemade bread into 13 perfectly even slices with this top-quality bread slicer crafted from solid wood. Attractive as it is easy to use, slicer measures 5" x 5" x 10".
#0554 Wooden Bread Slicer **$12.98**

 BONUS BUY! Order the handy bread slicer and get our *Homemade Breads* cookbook for just $2—you save $2.98!
#0555 Bread Slicer and *Homemade Breads* cookbook **$14.98**

COUNTRY HOME COOKING RECIPE BOX. Organize your recipe file *quickly and easily* in this solid-wood recipe box, specially sized to fit the larger-format "recipe cards" in issues of *Country Woman* and *Country*. Lid doubles as a handy card holder for at-a-glance recipe reading! Protective vinyl holders, sized-to-fit divider cards also available.
#5191 Country Home Cooking Recipe Box **$12.98**
#5192 Vinyl Recipe Holder Set (25 in set) **$3.98**
#5193 Index Divider Cards (12 in set)..**$1.50**

TO ORDER any of the above, or additional copies of *Pasta, Please* (Code 0206; $4.98 each), mail your order, along with your payment, to: Country Store, Suite 1977, Box 612, Milwaukee WI 53201. (Be sure to include $1.50 for shipping & handling for first item and 25¢ for each additional item.) Please...don't forget to include the code number for each item ordered—this helps us fill your order correctly and ship it without delay!